VIRTUAL FIELD TRIPS
in the
Cyberage

A Content Mapping Approach

SCOTT M. MANDEL

SkyLight
PROFESSIONAL DEVELOPMENT
Arlington Heights, Illinois

Virtual Field Trips in the Cyberage: A Content Mapping Approach

Published by SkyLight Professional Development
2626 S. Clearbrook Dr., Arlington Heights, Illinois 60005-5310
Phone 800-348-4474, 847-290-6600
Fax 847-290-6609
info@skylightedu.com
http://www.skylightedu.com

Senior Vice President, Product Development: Robin Fogarty
Director, Product Development: Ela Aktay
Acquisitions Editor: Jean Ward
Editor: Amy Kinsman
Cover Designer and Illustrator: David Stockman
Book Designer: Bruce Leckie
Formatter: Donna Ramirez
Production Supervisor: Bob Crump
Production Assistant: Christina Georgi
Proofreader: Peggy Kulling
Indexer: Candice Cummins Sunseri

© 1999 SkyLight Training and Publishing Inc.
All rights reserved.
Printed in the United States of America

LCCCN 99-71292
ISBN 1-57517-159-7

2459-V
Item Number 1746

Z Y X W V U T S R Q O P N M L K J I H G F E D C B A
06 05 04 03 02 01 00 99   15 14 13 12 11 10 9 8 7 6 5 4 3 2 1

This book is dedicated to my parents, Bernard and Audrey, who always provided for, encouraged, and nurtured my love for education and working with kids—even if it meant living on an educator's salary.

Acknowledgments

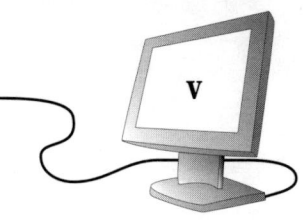

From beginning to end, and all of the stops in-between, many people had a substantial hand in the creation of this book.

First and foremost, I want to thank Jean Ward, Acquisitions Editor at SkyLight Professional Development, for sitting me down in her office last summer and saying to me, "Here is a book I'd like you to write. . . ." The pleasure of working with her on my previous book for SkyLight made me answer, "Absolutely!" and "How soon?" within seconds. Of course, one of my conditions was that I would be able to work once again with the wonderful editor of that previous book, Amy Kinsman. Her touch with my words and ideas made her an author's dream.

I would also like to thank a wonderful group of educator friends who reviewed my chapters as I wrote them and shared their ideas, insight, and suggestions on how to improve the work. Robert Schmuck, Jennifer Jones-Heroux, Michael Fishler, Melodie Bitter, and the new principal of my school, David Gonzalez, took time out of their busy schedules to assist me with this project. They are some of the best educators found in the Los Angeles Unified School District, and I am greatly appreciative of their assistance.

I also want to thank three people that got me hooked onto technology. The first, Gary Kelemen, my brother-in-law, introduced me to this great innovation called the Internet years ago. The second, J. B. Hiller, greatly assisted with the original construction of my Teachers Helping Teachers Web site and has constantly come to my aid when something goes wrong—such as when the Guest Book or the counter mysteriously disappears. Finally, I want to thank my technology partner, Jack Sterk, who has kept me up-to-date with the newest technology for the past ten-plus years, dating back to the time when Apple IIc's were considered technological wonders.

Finally, I want to thank all of the million-plus teachers and educators who have used the Teachers Helping Teachers Web site throughout the past few years. Your words of encouragement and support ultimately led to the formation of this book.

Scott Mandel

Contents

Preface ix

Introduction 1
   The Wonders of the Internet for the Classroom Curriculum 2
   A Step-by-Step Process 3

Chapter 1: Advantages of Virtual Field Trips 7
   The Human Experience: Adapting to Different Climates,
      Topographies, and Modem Speeds 7
   A Revolutionary Educational Resource 9
   Field Trips as a Curricular Enhancement 13
   Packaged Trip or Personalized Trip? 18

Chapter 2: Quick and Easy Internet Searches 23
   A Short Cut to Ancient Rome 23
   Easy and Efficient Ways to Locate URLs 24
   Search Engines and Directories 25
   General Education Sites 29
   Comprehensive Subject-Matter Sites 30
   Specific Subject-Matter Sites 32
   Teacher Guest Books 33
   Limit Search Time With Electronic Tools 35

Chapter 3: Plan a Virtual Field Trip Step by Step 39
   Team Time for Students 39
   New Learning Opportunities 41
   Determine Goals and Parameters 41
   Brainstorm a Model 44
   Investigate 47
   Make Decisions About Activities 54
   Address Assessment 64
   A Virtual Field Trip Checklist 66

SkyLight Professional Development

Chapter 4: Creating a Virtual Field Trip From Start to Finish 71
    Here Presenteth Thy Dilemma 71
    Putting the Methodology to Work 72
    Determining Goals and Parameters 73
    Brainstorming for Shakespeare 75
    Linking to Shakespeare 79
    Making the Final Decisions 87
    Assessing the Product 99
    Why Did She Spend All of This Time? 101

Chapter 5: How to Integrate Virtual Field Trips into the Curriculum 105
    The Shape of Society 105
    Where to Begin? 107
    Language Arts 108
    Social Studies/History 113
    The Humanities 117
    Science 120
    Mathematics 123
    The Arts 125

Chapter 6: Ready-to-Use Teacher-Created Virtual Field Trips 133
    A Trip to a Spider's Habitat 135
    A Trip Out of My Town 138
    A Trip in History to Visit Bleeding Kansas 140
    A Trip to Medieval Times 145
    A Trip to See the Work of Diego Rivera 147
    A Trip to a Weather Bureau 149

Appendix A: A Virtual Field Trip Checklist 151
Appendix B: Glossary 155
Appendix C: Index of URLs 159
References 163
Index 165

Preface

This book was written for classroom teachers, by a classroom teacher, and is designed with direct classroom applications in mind. The material on these pages is geared mostly for the advanced on-line user, the teacher who regularly incorporates Internet-supplied material into the classroom curricula. Use of the Internet as a supplier of curricular material—the ultimate teacher resource center—has become increasingly prevalent in the past couple of years. The virtual field trips described in these pages are designed to take the teacher to the next step, using the Internet as a teaching tool unto itself and as an integrated piece of the teaching process.

Virtual field trips can be as extensive or as brief as the teacher desires. The amount of preparation that is required is directly related both to the comfort level that the teacher has with the Internet and to the individual's goals and time availability. Please note, however, that the discussion within this book is explained step by step so that the experiences can be followed by all teachers, regardless of their previous experiences. Whereas some of the procedures appear lengthy—the creation of virtual field trips is quite simple once the teacher becomes familiar with the process. Do not let the amount of perceived work deter you. Look at the situation as being similar to the writing of lesson plans. For instance, in teacher preparatory classes, lesson plans are required to be long, extensive, and covering every conceivable aspect of the teaching experience. As the student becomes a full-time teacher, the lesson plans become more compact and ultimately contain only the information necessary for that particular teacher. The same philosophy should be applied and kept in mind with the material within these chapters. The more familiar and experienced the teacher becomes with creating virtual field trips, the easier and quicker they are to create.

Finally, the overall philosophy of this book is to *educate*, not *train*, teachers in how to create and integrate virtual field trips into their personal classroom curricula. The key is for teachers to learn how to adapt the material to their own personal teaching styles and educational environments and to make the material a natural part of their overall teaching repertoires.

Scott Mandel, Ph.D.
Van Nuys, CA 1999

Introduction

What would I see if I walked on Mars? What was everyday life really like for kids during pioneer days? If my house was under water in the ocean, what would I look at outside my window? Has anyone ever built a building shaped like a perfect sphere? These are all real questions asked by students. Typically teachers' answers start with the words, "I imagine you would...."

Thanks to one of the most stunning educational innovations of all time, the Internet, teachers can answer these questions with, "Let's go take a look." Thanks to the wonders of the cyberage, students can now travel to previously unseen places anywhere on Earth, outside of Earth, and back into history—places that were too difficult or simply impossible to visit a few short years ago. Any classroom teacher with a connection to the Internet can construct a virtual field trip for students.

Unlike many curricular innovations, these are not technological wonders that teachers can simply ignore if they feel uncomfortable with them. Quite the contrary. The "net generation" is putting new demands on teachers. Administrators, parents, and the community fully expect curriculum in today's world to incorporate this new

technology. These "digital kids" are already accustomed to the new type of interactive learning brought on by their increased use of cyberspace (Tapscott 1999). New national standards for creating technologically literate students have been recently developed for grades K–12 (Thomas and Knezek 1999). Although often overwhelmed with cyberphobia, teachers still must meet the demands of this new age. This book helps them reach this professionally mandated goal.

The Wonders of the Internet for the Classroom Curriculum

This is a book for classroom teachers, written by a classroom teacher. The purpose of this work is to demonstrate how everyday classroom teachers can fully and comfortably integrate the wonders of the Internet into their classroom curricula in a meaningful way. Too often online use in schools today is limited to the Internet-as-a-special-event syndrome, in which students complete a special project on the Internet that teachers may or may not integrate into the classroom curriculum. On the contrary, this book shows teachers how to use the Internet as a natural teaching device.

New research has found that the primary way to raise the use of higher order thinking skills through technology is *not* from the use of advanced software or hardware. Rather, success in this cognitive area is directly tied to the in-service work of teachers in technological literacy (Latham 1999). The focus throughout this work is to demonstrate to teachers how to design and implement virtual field trips into the everyday curriculum, taking students places previously unheard of before the advent of the cyberage.

This book is *not* a listing of virtual Web sites on the Internet. Nor is it a Yellow Pages of Internet resources. Instead, the material in this book demonstrates to teachers how to quickly and easily search for sites directly relevant to classroom projects. The following chapters take teachers through a detailed step-by-step process in conceptualizing, formulating, and constructing a virtual field trip for students—one that is directly tied to the teacher's curricular unit and is explicitly aimed at the ability level of these students of the net generation. Specific classroom examples are given in the major subject areas of the curriculum, from kindergarten through high school. More importantly, the ideas and examples are presented in a way to encourage their practical adaptation to teachers' particular curricular areas.

A Step-by-Step Process

The book is designed for the greatest possible ease of use for the classroom teacher. Chapter 1 discusses the reasons and logic behind using field trips as a curricular enhancement and explains the benefit of creating personalized field trips on the Internet. Chapter 2 provides a quickie primer toward finding materials on the Internet, describing search engines, directories, and taking teachers through the various categories of educational Web sites that exist today. Chapter 3 gets into the heart of the matter as it explains exactly how to plan for a virtual field trip and how to develop it so that it becomes a valid and meaningful curricular experience. Chapter 4 takes the information presented in the previous chapter and provides an actual step-by-step example of how to easily implement these ideas. Chapter 5 then goes subject by subject as it presents generic ideas of how classroom teachers can integrate virtual field trips into their specific curricula. Finally, to further demonstrate the ease of this process, chapter 6 provides a number of original virtual field trips in a variety of subject areas and age groupings provided by teachers from around the country.

A number of appendices follow these chapters: a virtual field trip checklist, a glossary of terms, and an index of uniform resource

locations (URLs) used in the book. For clarity, all Web site titles provided in the book are displayed in capital letters, unless quoted directly from a search engine listing. To keep these pages from becoming overly cluttered with long strings and numbers, all Internet addresses for sites listed in the text are found in appendix C, the index of URLs.

In all replications of search engine results, the bold title is a direct link to that particular Web site. The description that follows this title is an unedited reproduction of the description provided by the search engine and the text that teachers would read on their computer screens.

Now for the disclaimer: Due to the fluid nature of the Internet, by the time that this book is published, some of these URLs may be outdated, changed, or no longer in service. Never fear, for there are sure to be a least two or more new virtual field trip sources available on the Internet for every one that is no longer in operation. Chapter 2 demonstrates how to easily find this material.

ADVANTAGES OF VIRTUAL FIELD TRIPS

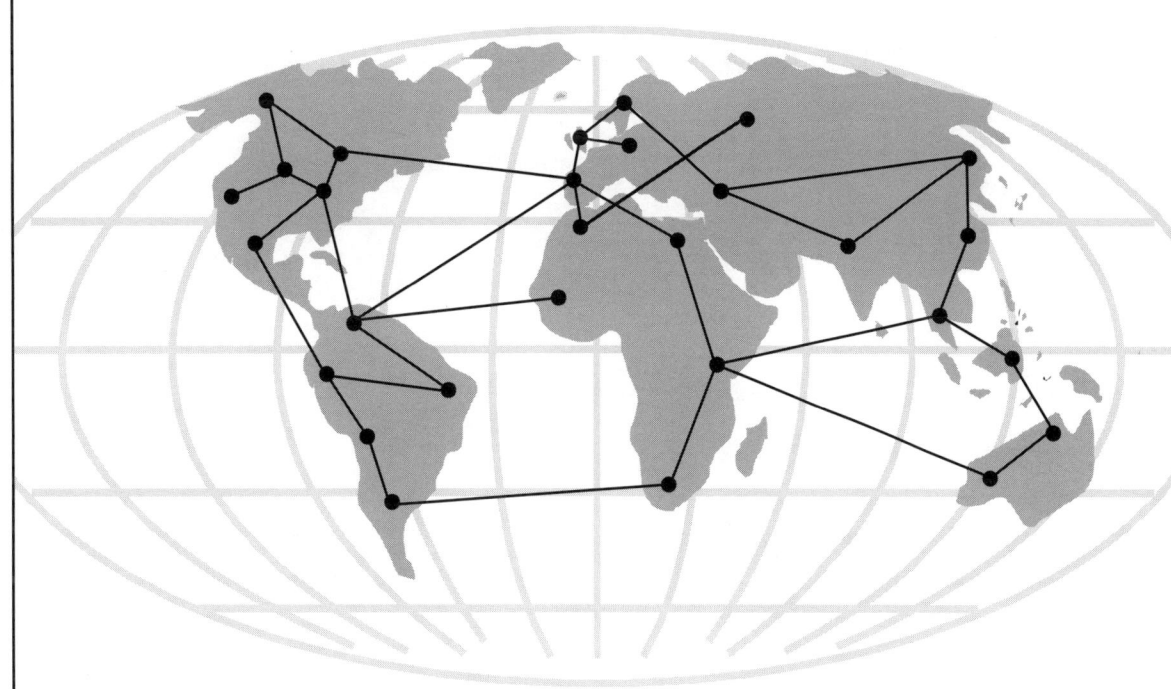

CHAPTER ONE

CHAPTER 1

Advantages of Virtual Field Trips

....

The Human Experience: Adapting to Different Climates, Topographies, and Modem Speeds

The high school students enter the computer lab and immediately move into their cooperative learning groups. Their topic of study involves an investigation of how people adapt to various climates and topography in their quest to create adequate living conditions. Within this particular cooperative learning lesson, the students' immediate task is to determine the types of clothing and equipment necessary to bring with them for a hypothetical trip to various spots around the globe. They must make their decisions based only on the climate and topography of that particular location. The source of their material is a virtual field trip experience using the Internet. The students are to synthesize the information and material they acquire into their overall study of human adaptability.

Prior to the session, their teacher, Mr. Lopez*, created a virtual field trip Web site and uploaded it onto the school computer network. The site includes links to previously selected Internet ad-

---

* All names of teachers are fictional.

dresses for locations that visually exemplify the material he wants his students to experience.

Each two-student team logs onto the Web site that appears as a weather map of the world. Various sites are designated as places for students to click on and visit. Each predetermined location on the map is linked to an Internet address containing a virtual Web site approximating the conditions the students would find at that particular location. The groups determine the various areas to visit, based on their personal choices. They each have a topic sheet that contains subject areas and concepts to search and answer, which forms the basis of a later classroom discussion. Some the various groups' experiences include the following:

Group 1
One group clicks onto the Bahamas and discovers a hurricane, thanks to the Web site USA TODAY WEATHER—A TYPICAL NORTHERN HEMISPHERE HURRICANE. At this site, students learn the meteorological steps involved in the development of hurricanes, see pictures of hurricanes in action, explore the long-recorded history of hurricanes, and investigate other variations of serious weather conditions such as tornadoes and thunderstorms.

Group 2
Another group visits one of the islands in the Pacific rim and explores an active volcano, courtesy of the site HAWAIIAN VOLCANO OBSERVATORY. This site presents students with pictures of various currently active volcanoes and the destruction they incur, especially from lava and earthquakes. The site also includes a section describing how volcanoes work and the general hazards posed by volcanoes to cultures that live in their vicinity.

Group 3
A third group faces the harshness of one of the world's numerous deserts through the Web site DESERT LIFE IN THE AMERICAN SOUTHWEST. The site describes in both text and pictures the status of various arid regions around the world, the animal and plant life that the region supports, and the fate of that particular area due to human encroachment.

SkyLight Professional Development

Advantages of Virtual Field Trips

Group 4
The last group investigates the unusual living conditions within the rain forests of Brazil, using the Internet site AN AMAZON ADVENTURE. The students study the various aspects of life in the heart of the rain forest, both human and animal. This particular site also allows students to take on the roles of explorers as they learn about life within that environment.

At the end of this Internet session, all of the students report that they have a significantly better understanding of the adaptability of different people to their environment. Much of this new perception is a direct result of their miscellaneous experiences on this virtual field trip of climates and topography around the world.

A Revolutionary Educational Resource

The Internet is often portrayed as either the largest-scale electronic toy ever built or the single greatest human convenience ever created. Many students see it as the ultimate toy: They can play online electronic games from around the world; check on an abundance of information concerning their favorite movie, television, or music star; and talk with their friends for hours in chat rooms or on the Internet Relay Chat (IRC). Whereas most adults see it as the ultimate convenience: They can access instant news stories, stock quotes, and sports scores; purchase almost anything from books to cars; and convey correspondence through e-mail at 1 A.M. without disturbing anyone.

Most of these online activities are significantly worthwhile, while others have a rather questionable value (see A Modern Convenience?). This phenomenon completely changes when one deals with the area of education. The Internet's greatest strengths have begun to manifest themselves in this particular domain. Over the past couple of years, this online resource has taken on a new role as the ultimate teacher resource center. Subsequently, there are two basic areas where the Internet has become virtually a revolutionary educational resource: providing learning opportunities previously unobtainable and allowing teachers to access curricular materials quickly and efficiently.

Learning Opportunities Previously Unobtainable

The Internet allows students to access information and materials that were previously impossible to acquire. Before the advent of the Internet, if students wanted to discover what was happening during a particular NASA space shuttle mission, they could realistically secure the information through a limited number of avenues:

1. Write to NASA directly and request the information. Students receive results in four to eight weeks, depending on the detail requested.
2. Read an account of the flight in a daily newspaper. The material is delayed by one day, and it may or may not have the relevant information that students want.
3. Watch a television news service, such as CNN. Although extremely up-to-date, the station may or may not be covering the particular areas in which students are interested.

However, in today's cyberage, students can now get almost any information they desire within minutes. For the above example, all they would have to do is the following:

Go online to the NASA Web site. Here students have immediate access to all the information about current shuttle flights. Included are actual shuttle pictures, details of the activities occurring on the shuttle, profiles of the astronauts, history of the shuttle, Web site connections to other materials connected with the mission, and many more informational opportunities.

> **A Modern Convenience?**
>
> The Internet provides everyday consumers with a number of conveniences. This electronic resource was of invaluable assistance when I was investigating new cars. I was able to shop around and look at models online, saving substantial driving time going from dealer to dealer. When I finally decided on a Saturn, I selected all of my preferred options from the company's Web site, determined the price, selected a payment plan, and then walked into a dealership with all of the information I would possibly need.
>
> However, the convenience of the Internet is questionable at times. I recently learned of a new uniform resource location (URL) that contains times for all of the local movie theaters. One Saturday night, I decided to use this new, modern resource to find the times for a local showing. I turned on my computer, waited for it to boot up, spent a couple more minutes getting online, then connected to the URL, and finally searched and located the pertinent information. Simultaneously, my son walked into the living room, picked up the morning paper, turned to the entertainment section and found the same movie time in about five seconds. Convenience?

SkyLight Professional Development

Connecting with NASA online inevitably provides materials that students would have significant difficulty in obtaining within a reasonable length of time.

The Internet can also have a direct impact on the classroom curriculum. Refer to the opening anecdote. In this example, Mr. Lopez incorporated the Internet within the curriculum as a means to expose the students to the properties and characteristics of various forms of climate and topography such as hurricanes, volcanoes, deserts, and the rain forest. The curricular opportunities that this new technology supplies are almost endless in the area of education.

Besides the electronic material provided by the teacher within the classroom, there are numerous other educational areas where students can individually secure information previously unimaginable. A student who is researching the culture of World War I can find lyrics and music for dozens of popular World War I songs online. A student who is doing a report on ancient middle eastern civilizations can access the Web site of the current archaeological dig at Megiddo in Israel and download pictures and explanations of the latest finds. This student can even correspond with the actual archaeologists working on the dig. Within minutes, a student working on an English report can find the literary location of every single reference that Shakespeare made to the concept of honor. It is mind-boggling when one considers the informational access the Internet now provides students.

Access Curricular Materials Quickly and Efficiently

The stark reality is that teachers often do not have either the time or the financial resources to access all of the supplemental curricular material that they would like to bring into the classroom. This is another way the Internet proves invaluable for teachers.

Consider a history teacher covering the years of the Great Depression. This teacher wants to supplement the curriculum by having students read the text of the first inaugural address of President Franklin Delano Roosevelt, in which he addresses a nation in the throngs of economic suffering. To obtain this obscure text, the teacher could search through the school library, then the public library, and then ultimately contact a social studies curricular resource. This teacher could even write the Roosevelt Presidential Library or the Smithsonian Institution to locate the piece. In

any event, chances are that either the teacher would have to spend hours trying to secure the material or would simply abandon the search, determining that the excessive amount of time necessary to locate the piece was not worth the short amount of time he or she would use it within the curriculum.

Instead, this history teacher uses the Internet to access the HISTORICAL TEXT ARCHIVE Web site. Within seconds of accessing this archive, this teacher links to a site containing the text of every single presidential inaugural address ever delivered, including "Franklin D. Roosevelt, First Inaugural Address."

Another example of the teacher benefits this resource provides involves a language arts teacher who wants to share with students a particular poem written by Robert Frost. Unfortunately, this teacher does not recall the title of the work. All the teacher remembers is that it involves a choice in life, represented by two roads. One option is for the teacher to search through various poetry books for the original source, using various libraries and resources, and to hopefully stumble upon the poem. Instead, this teacher searches the term "Robert Frost" on the Internet. Among the sites the teacher finds is ROBERT FROST: THREE VOLUMES AND C. At this site, the teacher selects the topic "Index of Titles." Unfortunately, the words "two roads" do not appear in any title. Undaunted, the teacher then selects, "Index of First Lines." Lo and behold, there on the screen is the line, "Two roads diverged in a yellow wood." The teacher clicks on that link and receives the full text to that poem. The entire process, from the initial search through checking both indexes, took less than five minutes. Chances are that it would have taken longer for the teacher to walk from the classroom to the school library.

Even a math teacher can access the Internet for material for the classroom curriculum. An algebra teacher who wants to locate supplemental materials for students—new, interest-sparking algebra problems beyond those the text supplies—visits the site THE MATH FORUM HOME PAGE. At this educational site, the teacher selects the link marked "Math Resources by Subject," then "K-12 Algebra," then "Internet Projects." The teacher finds the following additional sites and subject descriptions:

Ask Dr. Math - Archives
Middle school algebra questions
High school algebra questions

Advantages of Virtual Field Trips

Middle School Problem of the Week
Goals and Objectives: To challenge middle school students with nonroutine problems and to encourage them to verbalize their solutions.

Internet Projects for Algebra, Tim O'Brien
Four Internet projects and a unit on graphing linear equations created for an Algebra 1 class: Graphing Linear Equations; Adding and Subtracting Rational Numbers; Scientific and Standard Notation; Scatter Plot, Best Fit Line, Slope, Y-Intercept and Equation of a Line; Mean and Median, Stem Leaf Diagram and Histogram and Rounding. Each project takes approximately two days to complete.

MathMagic
MathMagic is a K–12 telecommunications project developed in El Paso, Texas. It provides strong motivation for students to use computer technology while increasing problem-solving strategies and communication skills. MathMagic posts challenges in each of four categories (K–3, 4–6, 7–9, and 10–12) to trigger each registered team to pair up with another team and engage in a problem-solving dialog. When an agreement has been reached, one solution is posted for every pair. Hosted by the Math Forum.

As teachers can see, there is a plethora of potential supplemental material in the subject area of algebra available on the Internet. Aside from having students use these sites, this teacher can have students participate in math projects networking with other students from around the country or around the world. The wonders and potential of the Internet provide an unique opportunity for an algebra teacher to easily go beyond the classroom curriculum.

Indeed, the Internet provides an unbelievable convenience to teachers. It provides learning opportunities previously unobtainable and allows teachers to access curricular materials quickly and efficiently.

Field Trips as a Curricular Enhancement

In the years before the cyberage, one of the few ways that students could extend their learning experiences beyond the classroom walls was through the use of educational excursions beyond the school grounds—field trips. Over the years field trips have ranged from being an intricate part of the

curriculum (e.g., a Sea Afloat excursion when studying marine biology) to a fun trip to the local amusement park to celebrate a sixth grade culmination. However, for the purposes of this discussion, the term field trip is defined as follows:

> A trip arranged by the school and undertaken for educational purposes, in which students go to places where the materials of instruction may be observed and studied directly in their functional setting; for example, a trip to a factory, a city waterworks, a library, a museum, etc. Syn. instructional trip, school excursion, school journey. (Krepel and Duvall 1981, p. 7)

A Valid Curricular Tool

Educators have conducted field trips in educational settings for a couple of thousand years. The great teachers Aristotle and Socrates used field trips in the education of their students (Krepel and Duvall 1981). Today, field trips are still an intricate part of almost every classroom experience starting in the kindergarten years. Field trips are limited only by the financial and physical access to the educational location.

In today's society, politicians and the community are stressing educational value and basing educational value almost solely on standardized test scores and adherence to concrete standards. Even field trips are now under a microscope as to whether they are curricularly worthwhile or a waste of classroom time and school money. Over the years, researchers have conducted numerous studies to determine the educational value of field trips. The overwhelming conclusion of the studies on the educational worth of field trips is that these outside experiences regularly provide significant gains in both cognitive and affective achievement for all students, at all grade levels, and especially for those students considered at-risk. (Rudman 1994).

As valuable as field trips are, simply getting on a bus and traveling to an off-campus location does not automatically ensure an educationally sound experience. Teachers must thoroughly plan field trips with specific curricular goals in mind, especially when teachers take into consideration the legal ramifications of taking students away from the relative safety of the school campus.

Advantages of Virtual Field Trips

According to the research, the more meticulously planned the field trip, the better it is both in curricular terms and in safety terms. Millan (1995) outlined ten basic factors that directly contribute to the success of a field trip:

1. The trip addresses the concerns of all stakeholders in a politically astute manner.
2. Reconnaissance trips can improve knowledge of the site and facilitate the trips in terms of both logistical and curricular considerations.
3. Teachers must link field trips to curriculum.
4. Field trips must fall somewhere between focusing activities and reflective activities, and the timing of trips is dependent on the particular course of study and on the previous experiences and abilities of the class.
5. All students must be able to participate in field trips, regardless of their physical, intellectual, or financial profile.
6. Field trips are successful if they actively engage students, both mentally and physically, at the site.
7. The closer to reality an experience is, the greater the benefit students derive.
8. Incidental learning is rewarding and is often an unexpected bonus, but safety is the first priority when the unexpected occurs.
9. The human resources available at a field trip site can contribute greatly to the success of a trip, and it is worthwhile to cultivate a good rapport with these individuals.
10. Oral and written stories, fictional or nonfiction, contribute meaning to the experience and increase student engagement.

Although not exhaustive, this list provides a basic structure teachers can use to plan curricular field trips.

Field Trips in the Cyberage

The Internet can extend the educational value of field trips to levels previously unimaginable. Virtual field trips, to or field trips taken online, can take students to locations too far away to travel or too expensive to visit. Virtual field trips can even take students back in time, into outer space, or into the microscopic world.

SkyLight Professional Development

VIRTUAL FIELD TRIPS IN THE CYBERAGE

A virtual field trip, if done correctly and in an educationally sound fashion, can provide many of the identical cognitive and affective gains that an actual real-life field trip can provide (Buettner and deMoll 1996 and Goldsworthy 1997). The trick is for teachers to give virtual field trips the same care and credibility as they would give real-life curricular excursions. Simply going to an interesting Web site does not constitute a curricular field trip in and of itself, just as an off-campus excursion to an amusement park would have limited curricular value. (Although, there are teachers who have attempted to justify a trip to an amusement park as a study of the gravitational forces exerted on the human body through the experience of a roller-coaster ride.)

Teachers need to give the same attention to planning virtual field trips as they would give to any other student trip. Virtual Field Trip vs. Real-Life Field Trip (see Figure 1.1) illustrates how the earlier listing of Millan's ten basic factors that contribute to the success of a field trip are equally applicable to the experience of a virtual field trip on the Internet. (See chapter 3 for a detailed explanation of how teachers can apply the various aspects.)

Virtual Field Trip vs. Real-Life Field Trip

Real-Life Field Trip	Virtual Field Trip
1. The trip addresses the concerns of all stakeholders in a politically astute manner.	*Applies.* Teachers must consider stakeholders, especially in today's politically sensitive environment with all of its concerns of letting students go online.
2. Reconnaissance trips can improve knowledge of the site and facilitate the trips in terms of both logistical and curricular considerations.	*Applies.* Teachers should visit the sites that they want to include on the trip.
3. Teachers must link field trips to curriculum.	*Applies.* Teachers must make virtual field trips curricular trips.

continued on next page

Advantages of Virtual Field Trips

Real-Life Field Trip (continued)	**Virtual Field Trip** (continued)
4. Field trips must fall somewhere between focusing activities and reflective activities, and the timing of trips is dependent on the particular course of study and on the previous experiences and abilities of the class.	*Applies.* Virtual field trips play the same curricular role as real-life field trips.
5. All students must be able to participate in field trips, regardless of their physical, intellectual, or financial profile.	*Applies.* Teachers must consider students designated as ESL, special education, and, even more so, those students who cannot afford a computer or home Internet access.
6. Field trips are successful if they actively engage students, both mentally and physically, at the site.	*Applies.* Successful virtual field trips need students to actively work through the experience, using their spatial and intrapersonal intelligences among others.
7. The closer to reality an experience is, the greater the benefit students derive.	*Applies.* Teachers should strive to create virtual field trips that let students see what they would see if they were actually at the location.
8. Incidental learning is rewarding and is often an unexpected bonus, but safety is the first priority when the unexpected occurs.	*Applies.* Incidental learning occurs naturally as students investigate linked sites. The safety issue here is more of a concern of students visiting inappropriate adult-oriented Web sites.
9. The human resources available at a field trip site can contribute greatly to the success of a trip, and it is worthwhile to cultivate a good rapport with these individuals.	*Applies.* Although the teacher is not in direct physical contact with individuals, it is possible to correspond with the Web site creators via e-mail, thereby obtaining additional information and sources relevant to the classroom curriculum.
10. Oral and written stories, fictional or nonfiction, contribute meaning to the experience and increase student	*Applies.* Supplemental activities after the virtual field trip enhance the experience as they would a real-life trip.

Figure 1.1

If teachers conduct virtual field trips in the same meticulous fashion as real-life field trips, students will acquire the same cognitive and affective gains that previous research has found. When this is possible, an entirely new world of experiences opens to all students regardless of the school field trip budget, as they can all experience firsthand the potential of the Internet as a valid curricular device.

Packaged Trip or Personalized Trip?

The entire concept of the virtual field trip is a relatively new one. Once teachers decide to integrate virtual field trips into their curricula, they need to decide if they can use a prepackaged trip or if they need to create a personalized trip to cover specific content.

Unfortunately, not many packaged online excursions currently exist on the Internet, and those that do exist are often filled more with glitz than with substance. Still, there is a growing number of online sites that teachers can incorporate into their curricula in some fashion. Packaged field trips generally fall into three basic categories:

Commercial Sites: These are sites that present a virtual experience in the hopes of either eventually selling the reader something, having the reader visit other commercial links connected to the site (where the products are sold), or getting the reader to physically visit the promoted location. An example of this type of site is a virtual excursion to Hawaii, such as IMAGINE HAWAII.

Informational Sites: These are sites usually prepared and maintained by organizations promoting a specific cause. These serve as a way to present their particular point of view to the public and to educate those who visit the site. Examples of this type of site are a virtual excursion to the rain forest or to other various animal habitats, such as A PAGE OF INFORMATION ON ELEPHANTS.

Educational Sites: Teachers or students construct these as classroom or personal projects. They cover a wide variety of topics. Although the quality of these type of sites vary, the hidden curriculum is significantly more limited than that in the two categories above. Unfortunately, one significant drawback to these sites is that their longevity on the Internet is often limited. A quality site that a teacher discovers one day may be gone the

Advantages of Virtual Field Trips

next due to the completion of that particular webmaster's class project. Examples of this type of educational site are an excursion inside a frog's body or a trip to a particular time period or historical event, such as A VIRTUAL GEOLOGICAL FIELD TRIP TO ICELAND.

Teachers can use all of these packaged sites with students if they can logically integrate the material into the curriculum. The benefit of using these sites is that someone else has already done a tremendous amount of the legwork and the online material is often of an excellent visual quality. The drawback to using these sites is that they frequently do not easily fit into the classroom curriculum. The sites either cover material that teachers do not want to cover or, more often, neglect to address the areas that teachers want students to experience on virtual excursions. In light of the limitations of packaged field trips, the only way for teachers to adequately cover all of the material that they wish to cover on a virtual field trip is through the use of personalized field trips.

In contrast to the packaged field trips, teachers develop personalized field trips through a variety of online sources to address directly the curricular goals of the classroom. With personalized trips, teachers create educationally sound electronic experiences that are fully integrated within the curriculum. The drawback to personalized trips is the initial time teachers need to spend researching relevant Web sites and stringing them together to form the trip.

The choice between using a packaged or a personalized field trip is similar to the choices made in the planning of a real-life excursion. If students go to a museum and take a predetermined tour supplied by that museum, with no alterations or changes based on their classroom curriculum, they would take a real-life packaged field trip. However, if the teacher talks to the museum personnel and has the tour tailored to meet the specific curricular goals of the class, students would take a personalized field trip.

Sometimes the packaged field trip, either in real-life or online, addresses the goals of the teacher quite adequately. More often it does not. By definition, the personalized field trip always addresses the curricular goals since it is designed by the one in constant connection with the goals and standards of the curricula—the classroom teacher.

The balance of this book shows classroom teachers how to design original, personalized virtual field trips that they can fully integrate into the classroom curriculum, based on standards and frameworks with assessments.

SkyLight Professional Development

Before teachers embark on this type of project, it is beneficial to visit some virtual trips that currently exist on the Internet (see What Does a Virtual Field Trip Look Like?). Teachers can find virtual field trips using any of the major search engines or directories (e.g., METACRAWLER, YAHOO!, LYCOS, INFOSEEK) and typing in the key words "virtual field trips."

Once teachers are familiar with the type of material to incorporate into virtual field trips, they can start to develop their own personalized virtual field trips. That is when the fun really begins.

What Does a Virtual Field Trip Look Like?

The following are a number of virtual field trips that currently exist on the Internet. Besides these, try some of the Internet sites that are listed in the opening anecdote. Obviously, a number of these online experiences are more sophisticated than most teachers need. However, these are good to get a feel for the kind of experience provided by a virtual field trip.

THE CYBERSPACE MUSEUM OF NATURAL HISTORY AND EXPLORATION TECHNOLOGY
(http://www.1nhm.org)
THE JASON PROJECT
(http://www.jasonproject.org)
THE LOS ANGELES ZOO
(http://www.lazoo.org)
MAYAQUEST
(http://www.mecc.com/internet/maya/maya.html)
MONTEREY BAY AQUARIUM
(http://www.mbayaq.org)
THE ROCK AND ROLL HALL OF FAME
(http://www.rockhall.com)
PLANETARIUM SKY THEATER
(www.starstuff.com/stars.htm)
THE WHITE HOUSE
(http://www.whitehouse.gov)

QUICK AND EASY INTERNET SEARCHES

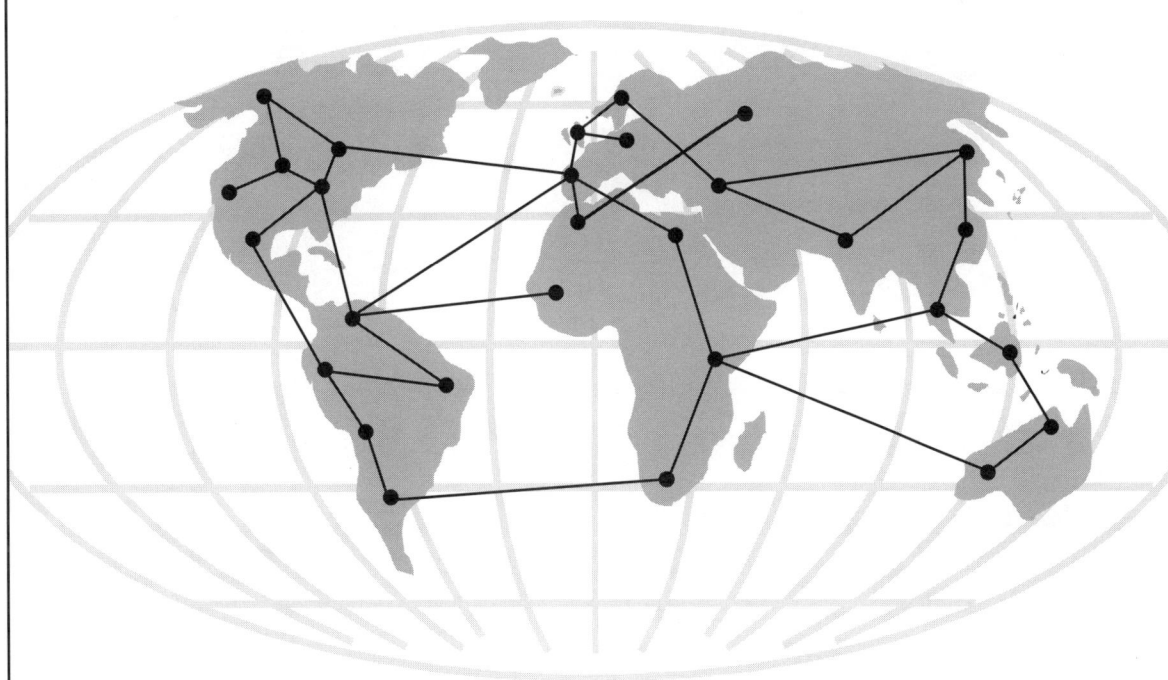

CHAPTER TWO

CHAPTER 2

Quick and Easy Internet Searches

A Short Cut to Ancient Rome

Ms. Johnson* is constructing a virtual field trip for her middle school students to visit ancient Rome. She needs to locate Internet sites that will visually take her students to different areas of the city and simultaneously expose them to some of the cultural aspects of the ancient time period. She first goes to YAHOO! and types in the search term "Rome." YAHOO! gives her a list so incredibly long, including many obviously irrelevant commercial or modern sites, that it will take her hours to wade through them all. Even when she uses the search term "Ancient Rome," she still receives seventy-five sites to examine. Again, simply by reading their descriptions, she deems that many of them are not educationally sound or appropriate for her needs. Then she remembers a great history Web site that someone had mentioned at an in-service session dealing with locating materials on the Internet. She cannot remember the exact name of the Web site, but she recalls that the person had mentioned that she found it through the TEACHERS HELPING TEACHERS educational Web site.

* All names of teachers are fictional.

Ms. Johnson immediately goes to the TEACHERS HELPING TEACHERS Internet site, finds the "Educational Resources" page, and scans down until she locates the section titled "History/Social Studies Resources On-Line." Within this section, she discovers the link to the site she was looking for: HISTORY/SOCIAL STUDIES WEB SITE FOR K-12 TEACHERS. Once she connects to this site, Ms. Johnson quickly locates the link "European History Sources," clicks on "Ancient and Classical," and then clicks on "Urban History." She immediately receives a list of educationally sound Internet sites involving material related to ancient Rome, including the following exceptionally relevant site:

S. P. Q. R. Welcome to the Forum
Virtual trip back in time to fourth century Rome. "Take a stroll through the streets and buildings of the Forum or participate in an adventure which leads you through the city."

This site is the exact type of Internet address Ms. Johnson is searching for to include in her own virtual field trip. She jots down the uniform resource location (URL) and incorporates the site into her students' online virtual experience about ancient Rome.

. . . .

Easy and Efficient Ways to Locate URLs

The most difficult and time-consuming part of creating a personalized virtual field trip is the process of locating all of the Internet sites necessary to include in the activity. Teachers use search engines or directories, such as YAHOO! or INFOSEEK, to locate Web sites. However, as Ms. Johnson discovered in the anecdote above, when it comes to securing educationally based curricular materials, using a search engine or directory may *not* be the most efficient way of finding information or Web sites. Too often teachers spend more time searching than constructing the trip.

Quick and Easy Internet Searches

There are many different ways to find miscellaneous types of Internet sites. The most efficient and easy way to locate such a URL is wholly dependent on both the goal and the status of teachers' searches. Some teachers who already have extensive experience incorporating online supplementary materials into their curriculum should have little difficulty with this process. However, this particular chapter is designed for the classroom teacher who does *not* have broad experience in locating various educational materials on the Internet.

The material in this chapter is presented in a general fashion so it is usable not only for teachers designing a virtual field trip but also for teachers trying to locate any type of online supplemental material for the classroom curriculum. The discussion centers around the following types of Internet tools: search engines and directories, general education sites, comprehensive subject-matter sites, specific subject-matter sites, and teacher guest books.

Search Engines and Directories

The initial place to begin any search on the Internet is with a search engine or directory. Since both serve relatively the same function, they are both referred to as search engines throughout the remainder of the book; however, there is a slight difference, which is explained below.

Search Engine Savvy

Search engines, such as INFOSEEK and LYCOS, contain an immense number of Web sites in no particular order. Think of it as a phenomenon similar to sorting thousands and thousands of papers alphabetically in one huge file cabinet system. To access the requested material, teachers simply type in titles or search terms and the search engine scans the database and provides links to all of the listed Internet addresses that include the individual search terms.

The benefits of using this type of electronic tool are that teachers can obtain a large amount of information quickly. Teachers may find some of the sites useful, most not, but teachers are not restricted to purely educational sites. The drawbacks are that unlike the phone books that various

SkyLight Professional Development

companies publish, in which each book contains every phone number within that area, not every search engine automatically contains every Web site on the Internet. A Web site author must first submit the site, which is subsequently approved and posted. Still, a search engine is sometimes the best place to start when teachers do not know how much material there is on a particular topic and want to get a quick scan of the possibilities.

The following is an example of an actual virtual field trip materials-gathering process. This particular subject is used throughout this chapter to exemplify the process.

Ms. Boyle*, a language arts teacher, is teaching the novel *The Crucible*, by Arthur Miller (1953). As part of the background supplementary material that she wants to provide for her students, she wants to create a virtual field trip back to seventeenth century Salem, Massachusetts witch trials. As part of her overall goals for this unit, she wants her students to learn about the lifestyle of that time period: clothing, houses, and other artifacts. This is in addition to learning about the historical facts of the events dramatized in the book. Since the material she has is not necessarily educationally oriented, she decides to start the process with a search engine.

Going to INFOSEEK, and using the search term "Salem, Massachusetts," Ms. Boyle receives exactly 228,023 links dealing with that particular term. Spending an average of just one minute looking and analyzing the usefulness of each site, she would get through them all in only 158 days (if she worked twenty-four hours a day). Not having that sort of time, she attempts to narrow her search to the "Salem Witch Trials." This time, she receives only 914 links—an improvement but still unmanageable. Therefore, she goes to a different type of search engine, METACRAWLER.

METACRAWLER is different from INFOSEEK and other search engines in that it has no database listings of its own. Rather, it searches all of the other major search engines and provides teachers with the top ten links from each, as well as those that contain the most or closest references to the search words.

Ms. Boyle conducts a search on METACRAWLER, using the original term "Salem, Massachusetts," which provides only nineteen links—a much more manageable number. The links include the following titles and descriptions:

---

* All names of teachers are fictional.

Salem, Massachusetts
Since 1626, Salem has been attracting visitors http://www.salemweb.com/ (Infoseek)

The Salem Witch Museum—Salem, Massachusetts
The Salem Witch Museum's presents the Salem Witch Trials of 1692, one of the most important and tragic events in American history. http://www.salemwitchmuseum.com/ (Infoseek)

Accused of Witchcraft
A listing of those accused in Salem, MA with brief histories of these victims. http://members.aol.com/samcasey/ancestors/witch.html (Infoseek)

All three of these are excellent places to begin looking for materials to use in a virtual field trip in connection with a unit on *The Crucible*.

Directory Differentiation

Directories are slightly different from search engines in that they separate linked sites into categories. Think of this process as similar to placing those thousands and thousands of alphabetically organized papers into specific subject folders within a file cabinet system, which are then placed into broader subject folders, which are in turn placed into subject file drawers, etc. In addition, most directories are much more selective about which URLs are posted. This is to teachers' benefit in an initial informational search. Teachers receive only the best sites rather than hundreds or thousands of sites with questionable quality.

The most well-known and most-used directory is called YAHOO! For the example above, Ms. Boyle could also have used YAHOO! first, rather than the INFOSEEK search engine. One of the strengths of YAHOO! is that it regularly lists all Internet sites that are related to specific geographical locations, such as the city of Salem.

Continuing with the example above, Ms. Boyle goes to YAHOO!, types in "Salem, Massachusetts" and gets ninety different sites, broken into specific categories. Some of the most relevant sites include the following:

Welcome to Salem, Massachusetts
Salem Massachusetts Architecture—in the 17th and 18th Centuries.

Salem Common

Salem Woods

Salem Witch Museum—dedicated to the Salem Witch Trials of 1692.

Salem Haunted Happenings—multiweek Halloween celebration that features parades, psychic fairs, costume balls, haunted houses, tours of Salem's great historic sites, and more.

Mary Bradbury's Trial—On July 26, 1692 Mary Bradbury was brought before the court of Essex in Massachusetts Bay in New England.

Petition of Accused Witch Mary Easty—from the Massachusetts Colony who in 1692 was falsely accused of witchcraft and executed.
Derby Square Tours—walking tours of Salem, including the Witch Trial Trails in October, geared to Salem's history, people and architecture.

It is quite probable that Ms. Boyle would have found all of these sites using the search engine INFOSEEK, but it would have taken an unreasonable amount of time for her to locate them. However, because YAHOO! is so particular with the sites it posts, Ms. Boyle may not receive many relevant sites.

When to Use

The differences between search engines and directories is usually quite minor. Normally, both are referred to as search engines. This chapter highlights the slight differences between the two to help teachers search more efficiently.

The basic rule for when to use a search engine and when to use a directory is as follows:

- If you know the exact name/title of a particular Web site, start with a search engine, such as METACRAWLER
- If you are looking for a number of unknown sites within a particular topic, start with a directory, such as YAHOO! If an insufficient number of sites are listed, either adapt the search term or try a search engine

Throughout the remainder of the book, the term *search engine* refers to both tools, unless YAHOO! is specifically referred to by name. Either way, if teachers want to locate a large number of sites on a topic and do not care if they are commercial, then a search engine or directory is the best place to begin.

SkyLight Professional Development

General Education Sites

A general education Web site is one that provides teachers with materials and information across the curriculum, substantially touching on every topic in education. These sites may contain lesson plans or other teacher resources. One extremely important component of these sites is that they inevitably contain numerous links to some of the best educational Internet addresses available for educators. In two situations following the use of a search engine, this is an excellent place for teachers to investigate:

- Teachers still need specific educationally oriented material after the initial search engine search
- Teachers have already determined that they can find everything they need on educational sites, rather than commercial sites

When people upload new Internet sites onto the Web, they regularly submit URLs to the top general education sites for inclusion on their educational links page. The authors of these sites, in turn, visit the submitted locations and make a decision as to whether to include the site as a link onto their pages.

The advantageous aspect about using general education sites when conducting research for a virtual field trip is that they have already filtered through the multitude of Internet sites that are produced weekly and have selected only the best to link to their sites. This saves classroom teachers hours of scanning through potential usable sites. When teachers use a general education Web site to find good links, they know that educators have analyzed the links and deemed them to be educationally sound.

Two of the best and most used general education sites are TEACHERS HELPING TEACHERS and KATHY SCHROCK'S GUIDE FOR EDUCATORS. Both of these sites have specific sections where teachers can visit and locate links to the best educationally oriented Internet addresses.

Continuing the previous example of the Salem, Massachusetts, virtual field trip, Ms. Boyle wants to investigate whether there are any educationally oriented sites dealing with this topic. Through her search engine work, she discovered a number of historical and cultural sites, enough to give students a feeling of the geographical area and time period. She now goes to the general education site KATHY SCHROCK'S GUIDE FOR EDUCATORS and looks at the "Subject Access" section on the bottom of the first page. She clicks on the link marked "History & Social Studies," and then

on the one noted, "American History Sites." There she finds the following links, all of which include educationally oriented material for her proposed virtual field trip:

Academic Info: U.S. History Home Page & Index
. . . a well-chosen list of links to support the teaching of American history; arranged by time period

Advanced Placement U.S. History Syllabus
. . . an absolutely awesome list of sites to support a full-year US History course arranged by time period and category

American History Sources for Students
. . . a briefly annotated list of links, classified by category

U.S. History
. . . an extensive list of North American history on the Net including books

While Ms. Boyle is at this general education Web site, she decides to also take a look at the "Literature & Language Arts" link since the core activity of her online experience is a work of literature. To her surprise, she finds the following site that contains an entire Internet-based supplementary unit based on *The Crucible:*

Language Arts Cyberguides
. . . supplementary units based on works of literature, designed for students to use with the Web

By using a general education site, Ms. Boyle narrowed her information search by immediately locating a number of excellent educational Internet locations that contain additional sources she can directly incorporate into her virtual field trip.

Comprehensive Subject-Matter Sites

Unlike a general educational site, which contains links to Internet addresses of every curricular area, a comprehensive subject-matter site limits itself to one particular subject area: literature, math, science, social studies, or the arts. Teachers who regularly use the Internet for supplemental curricular material can bookmark these sites on their browser for continual use throughout the year.

Comprehensive subject-matter sites operate in a similar fashion to the general sites. The authors of the site analyze and select the best Internet locations found within their subject field, saving classroom teachers hours of searching and analyzing on their own. Many of these sites are strictly educational, either produced specifically for teachers or as projects created by teachers and students. Being so narrow in their focus, many of them are not publicized on the normal search engines. Therefore, the only place to find them is through comprehensive subject-matter sites. Teachers can find the best of these locations through use of the general education sites mentioned above. Some highly recommended comprehensive subject matter sites in the major curricular areas include the following:

Language Arts: THE CHILDREN'S LITERATURE WEB SITE
Math: THE MATH FORUM HOME PAGE
Science: CODY'S SCIENCE EDUCATION ZONE!
Social Studies: HISTORY/SOCIAL STUDIES WEB SITE FOR K-12 TEACHERS
The Arts: WORLD WIDE ARTS RESOURCES

For investigating materials on the historical period covered by *The Crucible*, Ms. Boyle, the language arts teacher from the earlier example, visits the comprehensive subject-matter site HISTORY/SOCIAL STUDIES WEB SITE FOR K-12 TEACHERS. This site has one of the most extensive collections of social studies and history related material online. It contains thousands of sites on every topic imaginable within this curricular area.

To locate material relevant to the Salem witch trials period, Ms. Boyle selects the section titled "American History Sources." Once there, she selects the link to the "Colonial - Revolutionary" period. Among the 100-plus sites, she scrolls through are the following excellent links dealing directly with her virtual field trip topic:

The Massachusetts Enquirer
Mayflower, MA & New England Events, People, Life.

Witchcraft Hysteria
Studying the Salem Witch Trials.

Salem Witch Museum Education - Salem, Massachusetts

Salem @ nationalgeographic.com
If you lived in Salem, would you be charged?

Better That Witches Should Live
Biography of Thomas Maule who was acquitted of seditious libel charges after criticizing Puritan witch trials. Implications for the later development of the First Amendment.

By using a comprehensive subject-matter site such as this, Ms. Boyle located specific educationally oriented online material. She would not have easily found many of these links with a search engine, if they were even listed there at all. The authors of a comprehensive subject-matter site have completed much of the investigative legwork for teachers, giving teachers more time to construct virtual field trip activities, rather than spending hours upon hours searching for relevant materials.

Specific Subject-Matter Sites

A specific subject-matter site is a Web page devoted to one particular topic. Individuals who have a special interest in some distinctive subject, teachers or students working on a project, or organizations or groups that are promoting some distinct area or product normally create these locations. The majority of the links listed previously in this chapter (as a result of the various searches that Ms. Boyle conducted) are specific subject-matter sites. These URLs are the type of sites that teachers can directly link to a virtual field trip; these are the locations that contain the vast majority of the information or experiences that students will actually have during the Internet activity.

Teachers who regularly integrate the Internet into their curricula normally have a number of favorite specific subject-matter sites that they continuously use in their work. An American history teacher might have a favorite Civil War site, such as THE AMERICAN CIVIL WAR HOMEPAGE, bookmarked. A high school math teacher might have a geometry site, such as THE GEOMETRY CENTER, saved. THE ART TEACHER CONNECTION would be an example of a URL that an art teacher may have highlighted

Quick and Easy Internet Searches

on the browser. Internet-savvy teachers continually visit favorite sites with material that they can incorporate into every area of the curriculum.

Ms. Boyle, the language arts teacher from the example above, wants to use some historical documents in her virtual field trip. Therefore, she visits the specific subject-matter site called the HISTORICAL TEXT ARCHIVE. This Internet page contains full text versions of dozens of historical writings, most of which are not regularly included or easily acquired in either text books or local libraries.

Once Ms. Boyle links to the HISTORICAL TEXT ARCHIVE, she first selects the topic, "United States." Then she clicks on the link for "Colonial Period." Scanning down the list, she discovers a link titled "Salem Witch Trials." At this location, she finds the following links concerning this subject:

Salem, Massachusetts What about Witches?

Salem Witch Trials: A Chronology of Events

Discussion from Town Crier, including bibliography

A Timeline of Witch Trial History

The Salem Witchcraft Trials of Salem Village, 1692

Web Sites Related To Witchcraft Bibliography Project

Going through these sites, Ms. Boyle finds original documents, paintings, photographs, and explanations of the various events connected with this important period of history. A wealth of materials are available here that she can link to her virtual field trip. The added bonus is that much of the material covers items that she did not originally expect to find, much less include within the curricular experience. All of which, however, will greatly enhance her students' understanding of the period in which *The Crucible* takes place.

Teacher Guest Books

Finally, the last place to search for materials to include on a virtual field trip really is not a place containing actual materials at all. It is a place to get help and assistance through networking with other educators. Teacher

SkyLight Professional Development

guest books (sometimes referred to as electronic bulletin boards) are places where teachers can leave messages for other teachers, and where they can request help. Guest books normally contain room to type in any sort of request or question. They also usually contain a place where teachers can list their e-mail addresses, so that others can respond.

The relative ease for teachers to find materials for virtual field trips is wholly dependent on the original topics. Certainly, there are more than enough materials located for the example above concerning the Salem witch trials field trip. However, a teacher guest book is indispensable when teachers have difficulty locating certain materials.

One of the most used guest books is found on the general education site TEACHERS HELPING TEACHERS. This Internet site averages more than 50,000 hits a month and has an extremely active guest book. There are a number of retired teachers that spend a couple of hours a day answering calls for help that are posted on this page. The vast majority of requests that teachers post on the site receive between three and twenty responses within a couple of days.

At the beginning or during a search, teachers can put a general call for help on the guest book and let teachers respond. Ms. Boyle, from the previous example, put the following message on the TEACHERS HELPING TEACHERS guest book:

I am looking for sites for a virtual field trip to 17th century Salem, Mass., for the Salem Witch Trials (we're studying The Crucible). Any suggestions?

Within two days, she received twelve responses; some included new sources, some she already had listed. A couple of the e-mails included other suggestions, materials to consider, or offers of advice for teaching the unit (beyond providing Web site URLs). The responses include the following suggestions:

One of the sites I found was http://www.salemweb.com/ which is a homepage for Salem, MA. If you can't find more, maybe you could contact those folks for more info. TORONTO

As a Massachusetts resident, we get to take actual field trips to Salem. However, since you probably can't, try the Salem Witch Trials Chronology http://www. salemweb.com/memorial. BOSTON

Quick and Easy Internet Searches

I have a two-week unit that I did on The Crucible. If you'd like a copy, e-mail me your snail mail address and I'll send you one. LOS ANGELES

There's a web site called Arthur Miller's The Crucible: Fact & Fiction (http://www.ogram.org/17thc/crucible.shtml). Excellent background material there. Try it. CLEVELAND

The city was added to these messages to exemplify how this networking opportunity is widespread. Normally, this information does not appear in this location.

Ms. Boyle can follow up on this information or respond to individual e-mails to ask additional questions or to receive clarification. In any event, this electronic networking provides a significant source for material for classroom teachers.

Limit Search Time With Electronic Tools

The majority of time required to construct a personalized virtual field trip is spent on locating materials. However, if teachers know how to quickly and efficiently use the electronic tools available to find the particular information and Internet sites needed, they can drastically limit this search time (see Getting Ready for School, Morning Coffee, and the Internet). All it takes is for teachers to familiarize themselves with the advantages and disadvantages and strengths and weaknesses of search engines and directories, general education sites, comprehensive subject-matter sites, specific subject-matter sites, and teacher guest books.

The searches recorded above altogether took less than an hour to conduct. Whereas scanning and evaluating the sites takes longer, if teachers know the basic type of material they are looking for, the time spent is not overly burdensome. The educational rewards of virtual field trips for students are significant, as shown in the next two chapters.

SkyLight Professional Development

Getting Ready for School, Morning Coffee, and the Internet

While watching the morning news as I was getting ready to go to school, I saw a story on the violence in the areas of the former country of Yugoslavia. I suddenly had a brainstorm for a great lesson I could present on the human aspect of this tragedy with my class. However, I needed some material on this topic. It was also 7:05 and I had to leave for school by 7:25.

I immediately turned on my computer and let it boot up as I finished getting dressed. I took a second to press the Netscape button hooking me into the Internet as I went to pick out some socks. It was now 7:08.

I went into my bookmarks and selected Teachers Helping Teachers, clicked the Educational Links page, and quickly scrolled down to the Teachers Resources section, where I immediately found a link to the CNN Interactive Web site. I pressed the hyperlink and went to brush my teeth. It was now 7:10.

Since this subject was quite newsworthy at the time, there were a couple of relevant stories on the situation in the former Yugoslavia right on the first page of the CNN Interactive site. I found one that addressed the current situation, clicked on the link, let it load, and pressed the print button. I then went to get a cup of coffee. It was now 7:15.

With my cup of coffee in hand, I went back to the first page while my printer was working, found another relevant story on this topic and printed that one also. I then went to put together my school books and get my jacket while the printer finished. It was now 7:20.

At 7:24, the printer was done, I took out the pages, shut down the computer and headed to my car, ready to share the material and this new lesson I had in mind with my students.

PLAN A VIRTUAL FIELD TRIP STEP BY STEP

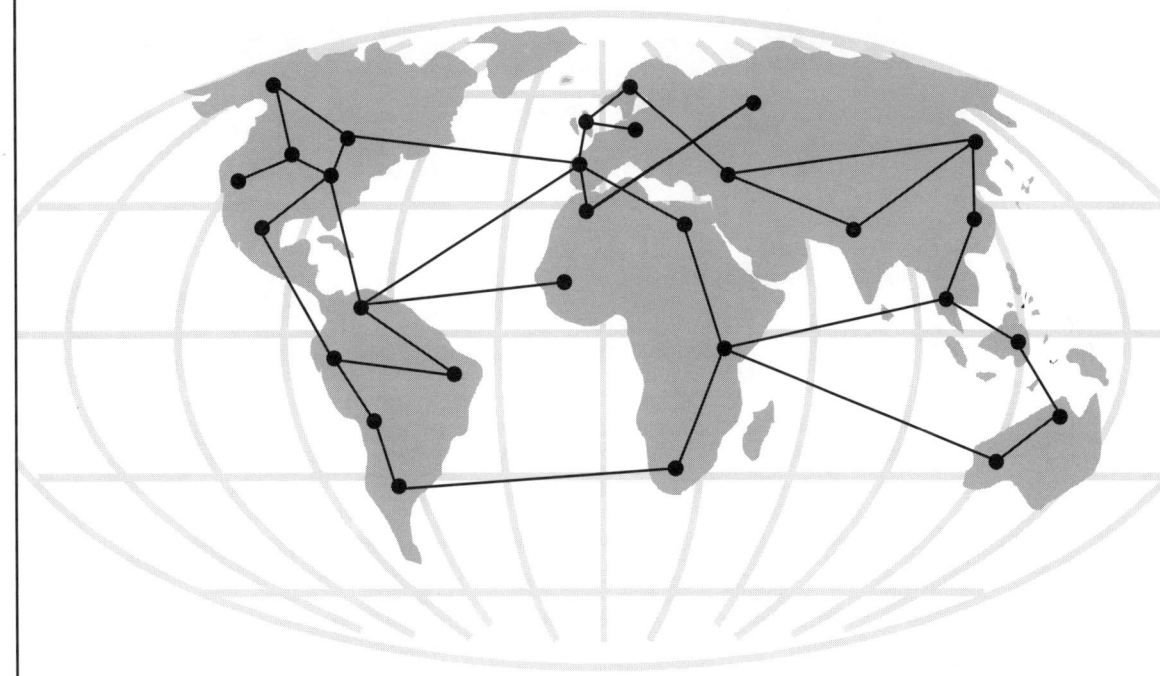

CHAPTER THREE

Plan a Virtual Field Trip Step by Step

CHAPTER 3

Team Time for Students

Mr. Lieberman* is experiencing intense frustration. He is having unexpected difficulty getting his high school students to understand the political climate surrounding the Boston Tea Party in 1774. His students are simply unable to comprehend the type of symbolic protest that occurred that fateful night in Boston Harbor. His eleventh graders are quite knowledgeable about the violent types of social protests of the 60s and the more recent urban protests in areas such as Los Angeles in the early 90s. They just cannot grasp the intricacies of the colonial protest movement. He decides that he is going to take his students on an Internet virtual field trip back in time to the Boston Tea Party. He will give them as much visual stimuli as possible to help them experience the mood of that era.

Mr. Lieberman's first stop is to investigate a variety of search engines and directories to see if someone else has already constructed a virtual tour involving this historical event. Unfortunately, all he discovers are tours for various science subjects (mostly biology and

---

* All names of teachers are fictional.

geology), an archeological dig, and virtual tours of both Hawaii and the White House. After a period of fruitless searching, he decides that he will have to construct his own virtual field trip back in time to the colonial era of the Boston Tea Party.

Using those same search engines, along with some educational-based Internet sites, Mr. Lieberman locates links to various historical and tourist-based sites to the Boston Harbor and the colonial period. Then, he quickly creates an itinerary page that contains a roughly drawn map of pre-Revolutionary War Boston and puts it on his school's Web site. He establishes links to the various Web sites he discovered, all of which are subsequently embedded within the map, in their appropriate location. Ultimately, the virtual field trip map of Boston contains the following material:

The Dock and Harbor—A link that includes pictures of a replica of the ship holding the tea, along with views of the harbor itself.

A Cargo Warehouse—A link that includes pictures and descriptions of the precise tea that was dumped.

A Newspaper Printing Press—A link that includes a diary of events of that night, in the order that they occurred. The site also includes copies of newspapers describing the events leading up to the Boston Tea party.

Various "Houses" of the Patriots—A link that includes background information and pictures for each of the main characters in the event. There is also an "inn" that includes the same information for other patriots of the time but who were not necessarily residents of Boston on that particular night.

The British Headquarters—A link that includes information of the British officers in charge and the British positions on this matter.

A Public Bulletin Board with Announcements—A link that includes parchmentlike copies of the original documents that inflamed the patriots such as the original Stamp Act, Tea Act, and Paine's pamphlet, Common Sense (although Paine's work was not written for another year, his ideas are still appropriate for inclusion).

Mr. Lieberman's students go to the school computer lab, open up the school Web site, and explore the event as if they were actually there. As a follow-up, they each write a letter home to relatives describing the mood and events of the night. Some take the roles of fellow colonists, some as British citizens writing back to England.

Thanks to the experiential learning available from a virtual field trip on the Internet, Mr. Lieberman's students come out of the session with a fresher understanding of the Boston Tea Party. As an added bonus to his preparatory work, Mr. Lieberman shares this virtual experience with his colleagues who are studying the same history material. Almost every eleventh grader in the school takes a virtual trip to the Boston Tea Party. Several local elementary school teachers adapt Mr. Lieberman's work for their fifth graders who are also studying American History. Mr. Lieberman saves all of the virtual field trip material to use the following year, fully integrating it into his standard history curriculum.

New Learning Opportunities

The power of the Internet as the ultimate educational resource center is becoming increasingly apparent to teachers as they create ways to extend new learning opportunities to students through this innovative medium (Tapscott 1999). Whereas creating a virtual field trip is significantly more work than simply having students find resources on the Web, it holds tremendous potential for giving them experiences previously unheard of, as documented in the example above. This chapter takes teachers through the necessary steps for creating their own virtual field trips, trips that are not only directly tied to their classroom curricula but are by themselves worthwhile and valid curricular experiences. The following chapter, takes teachers through an example of this process.

Determine Goals and Parameters

As was mentioned in chapter 1, the trend in education today is explicit adherence to curricular standards. Teachers are setting aside extraneous fun activities, such as field trips, unless they are directly related to a stated

curricular standard. Therefore, just as regular real-life field trips now require an educational justification, so too should those taken in cyberspace. It is sound educational policy and ultimately beneficial to both students and teachers.

Set Goals

The first step toward creating a virtual field trip is to determine the basic goals of the trip. Teachers need to tie virtual field trips directly to their current classroom curricula. Cyber-activities are just one more educational experience for students to acquire the material within a given unit. As a small test of whether there is a curricular connection, there are three rather basic questions that every teacher can ask before creating an online field trip:

1. *Why* am I planning this specific trip?
2. *What* curricular material will this trip cover?
3. *How* will this experience enhance students' learning in this unit?

The answers to these three fundamental questions form the basis for the trip. By asking "*Why* am I planning this specific trip?" teachers eliminate any noncurricular based online trips that they may come across. There are a number of interesting virtual trips to the moon available on the Internet. On the surface, having students enjoy and learn from a virtual lunar experience does not seem problematic. The dilemma arises if the science curriculum for that year is biology instead of space exploration. Although the moon trip may be fun and interesting, it has no curricular value, and the time spent on the activity may take away from other important topics.

With so little time to teach all of the material teachers need to cover, it is important to limit curricular tangents. Although this may sound terribly simplistic and basic common sense, it is an important issue to consider when dealing with virtual field trips, especially those that will amaze teachers when they first discover their existence. It is crucial to keep in mind that even though a virtual field trip to the inside of the brain may seem like a tremendous amount of fun and educationally rewarding, it may present significant consequences if it eventually contributes to not being able to cover all of the material in the physics class curriculum (see Looking Past the Personal Curriculum).

SkyLight Professional Development

Plan A Virtual Field Trip Step by Step

By asking the second question, "*What* curricular material will this trip cover?" teachers can avoid duplicating efforts and can begin to focus intensely on the specific subjects of the coming Internet search for materials. If students are already reading a play by Shakespeare in class, there is no reason to have them spend additional time reading one on the Internet. Therefore, teachers can ignore textual Shakespeare sites. However, if one of the curricular areas teachers want to cover is the experience of visiting the Globe Theater where Shakespeare's plays were originally performed, then teachers should look for Internet references to Stratford, England, and the Globe Theater.

The third question, "*How* will this experience enhance students' learning in this unit?" further crystallizes the curricular connection to the virtual field trip experience. There are a number of potential sites that would relate to the subject matter at hand, but not all of the experiences are worthwhile. An Internet field trip to the Los Angeles Zoo designed for elementary-age students, although interesting and well-done, may have dubious educational merit to high school students studying African culture. Teachers should not automatically include it just because it contains pictures of animals that happen to live in Africa!

Outline the Scope of the Trip

Once teachers determine the goals of their field trips, how the experience enhances their curricula, and how they will integrate it within their curricula, the next decision

---

Looking Past the Personal Curriculum

Recently, California divided the overall social studies curriculum into thirds:
- Fifth grade—Exploration through the Revolution
- Eighth grade—Revolution through World War I
- Eleventh grade—Post-World War I through modern times

Although both eighth and eleventh grade curricula allow for some review, the review is limited and some individual teachers discard it completely. This becomes extremely frustrating for other teachers on the faculty. If one eighth grade teacher spends three to four months instead of three to four weeks on the American Revolution, this teacher never covers the Reconstruction Period. Simultaneously, if a teacher at the high school does not conduct a review and starts eleventh grade history directly with the events leading up to World War II, a number of students who have both teachers never have the opportunity to study American History from the Reconstruction Period through World War I until they go off to college.

This is why it is important to not become so enamored of the wonders of the Internet that you focus valuable curricular time on one specific area. There are ample opportunities to give your students the same cyber-experiences while covering all of your curricular content.

SkyLight Professional Development

they need to make is the scope of their actual trips. How much of the unit does the trip need cover in this particular learning activity? Will the field trip supply the majority of curricular information, or will it be a side experience solely meant to supplement material previously discussed? The answer to these questions vary per unit. Whereas the geographical example in chapter 1 exposes students to the vast amount of material introduced in a geography unit, the Boston Tea Party example at the start of this chapter is a short supplemental activity to the larger study of the period.

Directly relevant to the scope of the trip is any student assessment teachers want to schedule either during or at the end of the unit. On a virtual field trip, one student may not cover the same material as another—unless the entire class is working on the activity simultaneously. Therefore, teachers must keep in mind that if they require specific, predetermined knowledge of material from students at the end of the unit, they need to provide additional ways to ensure that every student has the opportunity to cover the material. If teachers want to assess students on the material from the virtual field trip, then they need to include assessment that involves some type of open-ended higher order thinking format. This allows students to share their individual experiences and concepts that they attained. (See Addressing Assessment at the end of this chapter for more detailed information on assessment.)

The assessment of the unit is critical to keep in mind as teachers begin to formulate field trip experiences, especially since at least one student will raise his or her hand and ask, "Will this stuff be on the test?"

Brainstorm a Model

Virtual field trips, for the most part, are uncharted curricular territory. That is, there are few models of how to design one or what to do while experiencing one. Unlike most curricular units, there are few examples of virtual field trips that teachers have already conducted—models that other teachers can easily adapt to their own particular goals. Those trips that do exist are primarily limited to the area of the sciences. Therefore, since there is little to guide a teacher, it is imperative that in the initial stages of planning virtual trips, teachers conduct brainstorming sessions. Teachers can conduct these sessions alone or with other teachers. The important part of these sessions is to create an initial web of possibilities and to check those possibilities for viability and practicality.

Web the Possibilities

Most language arts teachers conduct brainstorming exercises with their students on a continual basis. There are a variety of brainstorming activities to choose from, but probably the best one in this situation is a web of possibilities. (Do not confuse the term with the nickname for the World Wide Web or Internet.)

Webbing allows teachers to put down on paper every idea that comes to their minds and to visualize and follow the connections leading from one idea to another. It allows teachers to consider every possible idea even remotely connected to the topic at hand. At this point, do not reject any ideas. Every association between ideas is represented by a line. This shows basic connections from one curricular activity or topic to another. This exercise is extremely appropriate to a virtual field trip as this connecting process mirrors the process of following one link to another while on the Internet (see Figure 3.1).

To begin a virtual field trip web, teachers place basic topic areas within a small circle in the middle of a large blank sheet of paper. Next, they connect the goals (the ones determined in the previous section) to the topic. Finally, teachers start thinking of every curricular activity possible in connection with those goals, letting one idea lead to another, and write down every thought they formulate. Teachers should not yet evaluate the ideas; that step comes later. This webbing activity is simply a worksheet—a collection of miscellaneous possibilities.

Check for Viability and Practicality

Once teachers exhaust their creativity, they can check each of the various ideas to determine its viability. First, teachers ensure that every idea listed truly matches the goals. If not, they need to either discard the activities or adapt the goals. Changing goals is perfectly acceptable as new ideas or situations arise that teachers feel would enhance students' learning. Teachers should still ensure that the new goals meet their curricular standards.

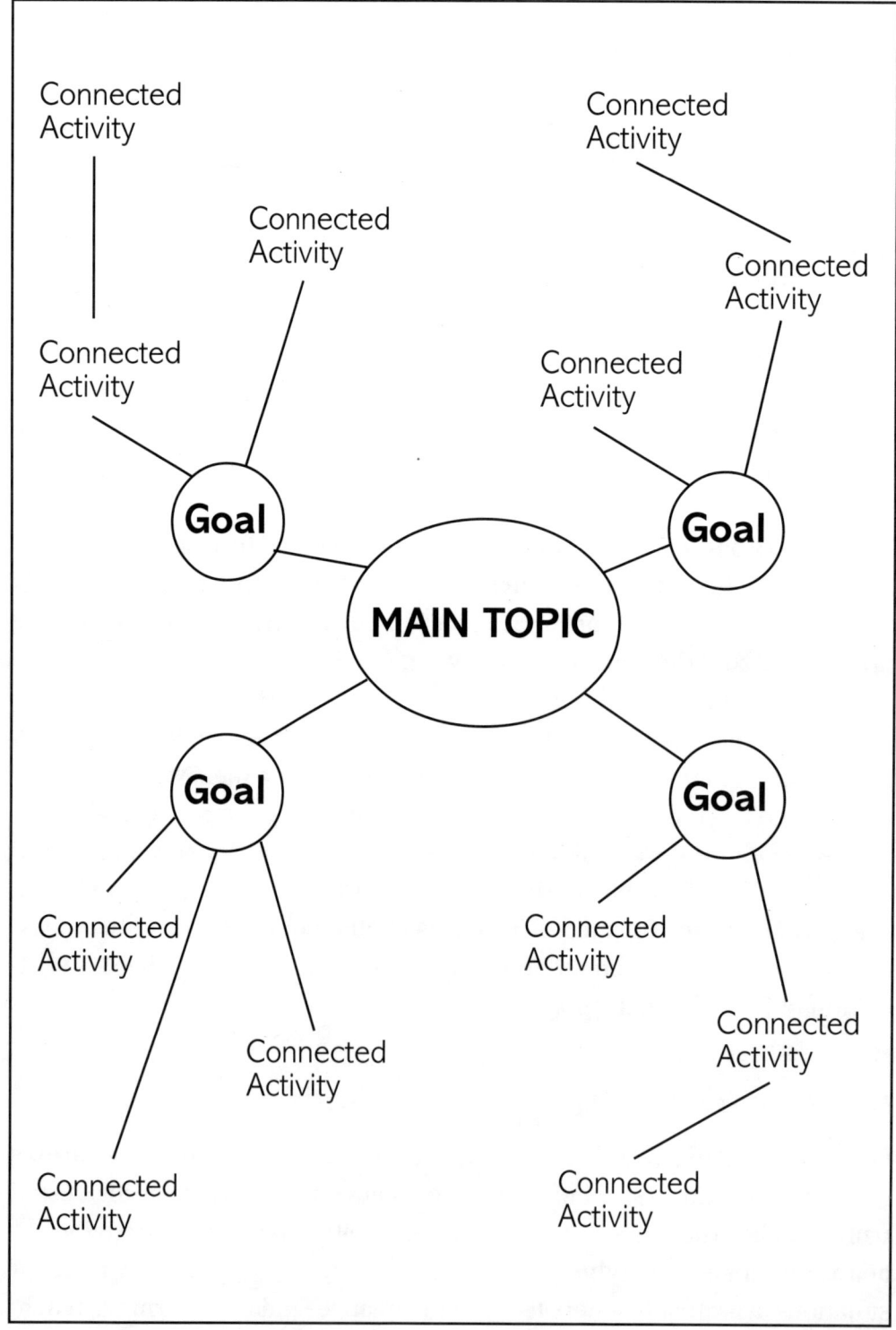

Figure 3.1

Next, teachers need to check for practicality. Teachers must take into account classroom or lab time available for their virtual field trips, the age and abilities of the students, and the material resources at hand. It is impractical to have a virtual field trip with twenty-five potential "stops" when the class only has an hour to spend in the computer lab.

Once teachers eliminate impractical activities, they can rewrite their original webs, citing only the planned stops for the virtual field trip. At this point, teachers can now search for Web sites that will provide material for each activity on the trip. This rewritten sheet provides teachers with areas they can plug in the various goals and connected activities and have space to write in Web sites or URLs. (See Figure 3.2 for a diagram of the entire webbing process for virtual field trips.)

Investigate

Teachers spend the vast majority of their virtual field trip planning time on investigating Internet sites to include on their trips. This section uses the material presented in the previous chapter and directly relates it to the construction of a virtual field trip.

Look for Existing Virtual Field Trip Sites

The first step in the investigation is to locate virtual Internet sites that already exist. After all, there is no value in re-creating the wheel. Teachers can find a number of commercial virtual sites on the Internet; although, as mentioned earlier, the vast majority of them are limited to the sciences or present-day locations for people to actually visit. A virtual field trip site such as ADVENTURE ONLINE is an example of a commercial site—a site created by a business with the goal of having the reader ultimately buy a product, service, or in this case, a subscription to the full educational material that they provide. A search engine usually provides listings for most of these types of commercial sites.

Another excellent source of virtual Web sites are schools. Many teachers have their students do virtual field-trip–type sites as a project and then upload them onto the Internet (see School-Made Web Sites). Again, the majority of these show up on a METACRAWLER search or teachers can find them on various educational or subject-matter sites that contain links to schools.

SkyLight Professional Development

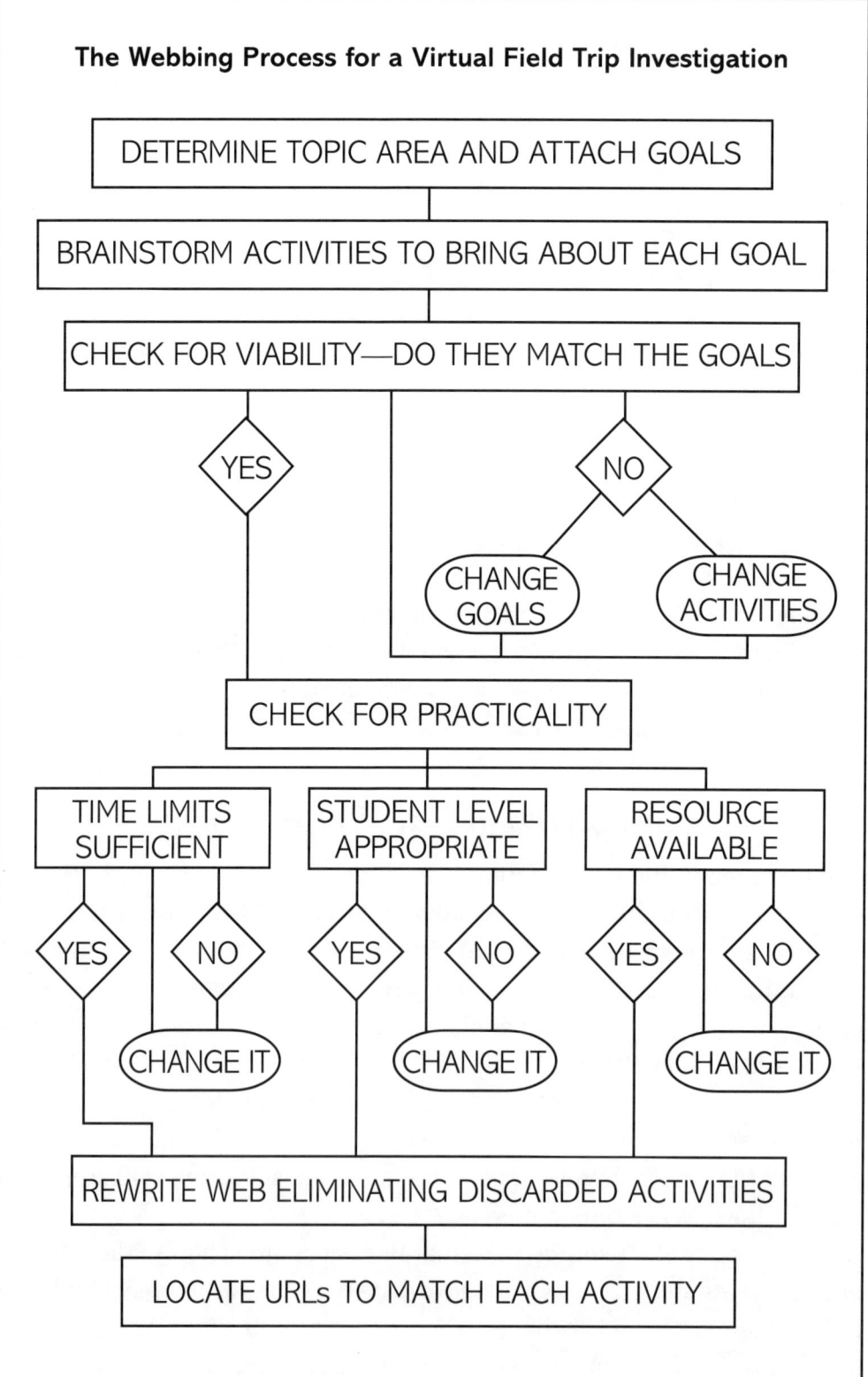

Figure 3.2

Plan A Virtual Field Trip Step by Step

Say that a teacher wants to do a virtual field trip on rain forests—a very popular topic for all grade levels and one that has extensive material on the Internet (see School-Made Web Sites). The teacher uses METACRAWLER to search the term rain forest and receives the following links and descriptions:

Rain forest Alliance Home Page
WebCrawler: Learn about the Rain Forest Alliance. Hop over to our marketplace where you'll find T-shirts, boxers, earrings & much more! A percentage of sales from this section of the site go to benefit Rain Forest Alliance conservation programs.
http://www.rainforest-alliance.org/
(WebCrawler Excite Infoseek)

! Australian wildlife ! rain forest birds, mammals, reptiles,...
WebCrawler: Photographs and detailed information on Australian rain forest birds, marsupials, mammals, reptiles, frogs, butterflies in Tropical North Queensland. Courtesy of Chambers Wildlife Rain forest Lodge. Courtesy of Chambers Wildlife Rain Forest Lodge. Yahoo!: near Lake Eacham, in cool, tropical highland rain forest.
http://www.wildlife-australia.com/
(WebCrawler Excite Yahoo!)

> **School-Made Web Sites**
>
> Always be cautious when planning to use virtual field trips created by students or teachers in other schools. The problem is that these sites disappear quite frequently, with little or no advance notice, as the authors of the site move on to new projects. This can become rather problematic if students are in the computer lab about to use an Internet site that no longer exists. Check out the viability of all links within twenty-four hours of introducing them to students.
>
> If you are planning on using a site created by another school, it is always a good idea to either copy down for future reference the URLs that the site uses or e-mail the school for permission to download the html for the site or store the site in the computer's cache. This way you have the material accessible even if that particular site is taken off of the Internet.

GeoCities - RainForest
Explore The Suburbs: Lost in the jungle? The RainForest Community Website is a virtual survival guide for the natives of the RainForest. Do you want to keep up with environmental issues and what's going on in RainForest here at GeoCities?
http://www.geocities.com/rainforest/ (WebCrawler)

Rain Forests Directory, Rain Forests, Ecology, Directory, Guide, Yellow Pages, Index, ...
A Complete Rain Forests Directory, Rain Forests Guide, and Index of related Links http://www.ahandyguide.com/cat1/r/r350.htm (Infoseek)

SkyLight Professional Development

As shown, there are already an abundance of virtual sites that deal with a virtual trip to the rain forest. Therefore, this teacher would waste a significant amount of time creating a virtual online excursion, when excellent ones already exist.

Unfortunately, the chances of finding an Internet site that provides a virtual field trip that happens to cover the particular goals teachers have already formulated is slim at best. Teachers must conduct their own investigation of the Internet in the search for potential places for their students to visit.

Use Search Engines to Find Material

A real-life field trip normally involves examining various artifacts, or it includes student participation in a variety of activities (similar to viewing multiple rooms or exhibits within a museum). Teacher-constructed cybertrips must involve a variety of Web sites that together cover the activities outlined in the planning activity above. It is extremely rare that only one or two sites will provide all of the activities listed on the goal sheet. Ultimately, teachers must move from activity to activity when searching for potentially useful Internet locations.

There is a natural progression teachers can take when conducting this sort of investigation—one that makes the most efficient use of teachers' valuable time. The following explanation moves from the most useful, less time-consuming search processes to those that may take longer to provide all of the information necessary for the construction of a virtual field trip.

Make Use of Metacrawler

Teachers can first try the search engine METACRAWLER. As is discussed in chapter 2, the wonderful quality of METACRAWLER is that it searches the top search engines and directories and provides the top ten links. Since not every search engine lists each URL, teachers conduct a hit and miss proposition when they use a particular search engine. If METACRAWLER does not provide any matches, it is highly unlikely that any one particular search engine would be more helpful. In addition, by limiting the search to the main Internet sites that contain the given search term, teachers do not have to wade through potentially thousands of Web sites that may remotely contain the term.

Plan A Virtual Field Trip Step by Step

Mr. Hughes* wants to take his students on a virtual field trip to the Battle of Gettysburg. He has already determined that there is not a preexisting site available online for this activity, so he needs to construct his own. In formulating his goals, he has already planned on including a number of initial activities such as the following:
- A detailed description of the battle
- An investigation of the personalities involved in the conflict
- Examples of clothes, weapons, and basic culture from that time period

A METACRAWLER search using the term "Gettysburg" provides a number of relevant Internet sites, including the following useful links and descriptions:

The Unofficial Visitors Guide to Gettysburg
WebCrawler: The Unofficial Visitors Guide to Gettysburg is a complete visitors guide to the Gettysburg battlefield featuring hundreds of photos of the Gettysburg battlefield, battle diaries and links to other Civil War and Gettysburg sites.
Yahoo!: guide to the Gettysburg battlefield, local accommodations, and attractions.
http://www.gettysburgguide.com/ (WebCrawler, Excite, Yahoo!)

Welcome To Main Street Gettysburg
history, civil war, Gettysburg, Pennsylvania, main, street, tourist
http://www.visitgettysburg.com/mainstreet/msghome.htm (WebCrawler)

Library of Congress Online Exhibitions
Dresden: Treasures from the Saxon State Library. Women Come to the Front : Journalists, Photographers, and Broadcasters During WWII. Creating French Culture : Treasures from the BibliothËque nationale de France
http://lcweb.loc.gov/homepage/exhibits.html (WebCrawler)

These links are only three of the most useful sites out of the fifty links that METACRAWLER provided in this particular search. Once Mr. Hughes quickly investigates the sites on his screen, he can then decide on a couple of options. First, he can look for more sites, using additional search engines and directories, or he can narrow his search to education-oriented URLs.

* All names of teachers are fictional.

SkyLight Professional Development

Search Educational Sites for Additional Material

The next place to investigate is a general educational site such as TEACHERS HELPING TEACHERS or KATHY SCHROCK'S GUIDE FOR EDUCATORS. As described in the previous chapter, both of these sites contain extensive educational links pages. Mr. Hughes first goes here to easily locate subject-matter Internet sites that contain the educational information he seeks.

In the History/Social Studies Resources On-Line section of the Educational Resources page of TEACHERS HELPING TEACHERS, there is the previously mentioned Web site titled the HISTORY/SOCIAL STUDIES WEB SITE FOR K-12 TEACHERS. This is one of the best subject-matter educational sites online. The site contains thousands of links covering the best Internet sites available in the various curricular areas of social studies and history.

Once linked to this site, Mr. Hughes selects "American History Sources," then "The Civil War" to investigate Gettysburg-related Web sites at this location. The search provides approximately 200 educationally oriented Civil War pages on the Internet, including the following links and descriptions, all of which meet some of the above-stated goals for the proposed virtual field trip:

The American Civil War Homepage
One of the more comprehensive and well-organized pages on the topic.

American Civil War Ethnography-Home
A page dedicated to examining the culture that existed in the United States during the Civil War using primary source materials from that time period.

Civil War Interactive
Dine on the Civil War. Interested in making an Irish Stew for 50 people ?? Find out how here.

By incorporating general and subject-matter educational Internet sites, Mr. Hughes can locate a substantial number of locations from which to create the virtual field trip. However, if he still wants *more* locations to investigate or has still not found exactly what he wants, he can network with other teachers around the country and around the world through the use of a teacher guest book.

SkyLight Professional Development

Plan A Virtual Field Trip Step by Step

Teacher guest books are places where teachers can post questions for each other and provide an e-mail address linked to that request. As was mentioned earlier, one of the most popular ones is the guest book on the general education site TEACHERS HELPING TEACHERS. This particular guest book is read by hundreds of teachers every day. The majority of requests for information on this site ultimately receive between three and fifteen responses.

Continuing with the Gettysburg example, Mr. Hughes places the following message in the guest book of TEACHERS HELPING TEACHERS:

> I am constructing a virtual field trip on the Internet for students to experience the Battle of Gettysburg. Does anyone have any good Civil War sites they can recommend that would enhance their understanding of this period? I'm looking for sites with pictures and information about the battle, the people, and the culture at that time. Thanks!

The first response to the e-mail came exactly forty-five minutes after he posted the request. Within two hours, other teachers had sent four responses to the request for information. Within two days, Mr. Hughes receives a total of eleven e-mails with messages that include the following excellent resources:

> Have you tried the American Memory site of the Library of Congress? **(http://lcweb2.loc.gov/ammem/amhometxt.html)**
> They have photos, WPA transcripts of interviews, film clips, and music/songs, although you may have to do a little hunting to find exactly what you need.

> **http://www.execpc.com/~dboals/a-part1.html#THE CIVIL WAR**
> I checked this out and there are some good links with descriptive headings.

> Have them take a look at **www.historychannel.com** for a day-by-day look at the civil war and links.

> Great Gettysburg site
> **http://www.mindspring.com/~murphy11/getty/**

Through the systematic use of search engines and directories, general and subject-matter educational Web sites, and networking with other teachers using guest books, teachers can easily acquire all of the information they need to create excellent virtual field trips (see Figure 3.3).

SkyLight Professional Development

> **Steps to Take When Searching for Web Sites**
>
> - Use METACRAWLER. If a number of links are provided (over fifty) and more are desired, look at the following search engines and directories: ALTA VISTA, EXCITE, INFOSEEK, LYCOS and YAHOO! If less than fifty links are provided, or if you are not able to locate enough educational Internet sites, go to the next step.
>
> - Use a general educational site such as TEACHERS HELPING TEACHERS or KATHY SCHROCK'S GUIDE FOR EDUCATORS. Both of these sites contain extensive educational links pages that can easily and immediately lead you to more specific, subject matter educational sites involving your topic.
>
> - Put a message in a teacher guest book such as the one found on TEACHERS HELPING TEACHERS. Many other teachers may have already located online sites similar to the curricular area for which you are searching. By leaving a message, you may get a number of e-mail suggestions that will fulfill your search needs.

Figure 3.3

Make Decisions About Activities

Once teachers investigate and collect a number of Internet sites to incorporate into their virtual field trips, they can plot them on their webs. Using the previous Gettysburg example, Figure 3.4 provides a small-scale example of what Mr. Hughes' web looks like at this stage of the process.

After teachers complete the initial planning and investigating, they can make specific decisions regarding the curricular material that they gathered. These are the same type of decisions that teachers contemplate whenever they want to integrate a new learning activity into the basic classroom curriculum. The areas of question involve the following:

- Analyze the appropriateness of the collected sites
- Reevaluate the goals and activities of the virtual field trip
- Make a logical plan to implement the virtual field trip into the curriculum
- Check for use of the multiple intelligences theory

Plan A Virtual Field Trip Step by Step

Battle of Gettysburg

Events of the Battle
Pictures of battlefield, locations, soldiers copies of letters
(American Memory
lcweb2.loc.gov/ammem/amhometxt.html)
(Unofficial Visitors' Guide to Gettysburg
GettysburgGuide.com)

Culture
The Arts
(Poetry and Music of the Civil War
erols.com/kfraser)
(Music of the Civil War
geocities.com/SouthBeach/
Boardwalk/2575/civil.html)
Food
(Civil War Cookbook
almshouse.com/cookbook.htm)

Weapons
Pictures of weapons
(American Memory
web2.loc.gov/ammem/amhometxt.html)
(Handguns of the Civil War
mntnweb.com/hobby/gun/index.htm)

BATTLE OF GETTYSBURG

Lifestyle
Attitudes of People/Family Splits
(The Civil War Years
jefferson.village.Virginia.EDU/
vshadow2/cwhome.html)

The Gettysburg Address
Picture of Cemetery—location of speech
(American Memory
lcweb2.loc.gov/ammem/amhometxt.html)
Text of the Speech
(The Gettysburg Address
msstate.edu/Archives/History/USA/19th_C./
gettysburg-address)

Figure 3.4

Analyze the Appropriateness of the Collected Sites

Once teachers collect all of the Internet sites for students to visit, they must analyze each site for its appropriateness. There are two important components of this analysis: a careful examination of the material within the sites and a look at the actual loading of the site.

Examine the material

Teachers, knowing their students and community, need to decide on the following:
- The appropriateness of the subject material within the site
- The language level of the material

Of course, Web sites containing graphic pictures of violence or adult subject matter are highly inappropriate for elementary students. Teachers must also consider the particular culture of the community when examining material. A Civil War site glorifying the North would most likely be inappropriate for use in a Southern school that views the Civil War quite differently than schools in other parts of the United States. A link to a site that has references to gay issues may be acceptable to a metropolitan school district but not to one in a rural, conservative area. Similarly, material alluding to a creationist point of view in science would be much more agreeable to schools in the deep, religious South than in the industrial, secular North. Teachers need to be cognizant of the intellectual and emotional levels of the students and the mores of the community. It is inevitable that anything deemed even *somewhat* controversial will make its way into the dinner conversations of many of the students that night. With community activism in education as prevalent as it is today, teachers need to keep this in mind when going through the final selection of sites they are going to use in virtual field trips.

Another basic decision that teachers need to contemplate is the appropriateness of the language level used throughout the material. Unless teachers are personally directing the whole class through field trips (i.e., going from graphic to graphic and providing explanation), they need to ensure that any online narratives or descriptions are within acceptable boundaries for the particular level of students. This applies to both higher- and lower-level students. Written material that is eminently difficult frustrates young students; likewise, written material that is aimed at younger students makes secondary students consider the virtual field trip as if it were a joke. Neither attitude is conducive for a rewarding educational experience for students, negating the basic goal of the entire Internet activity.

SkyLight Professional Development

Test load time

Teachers also need to conduct an analysis of the physical loading of the site. Extensive loading times frustrates students and provides them with substantial off-task periods. This not only becomes a waste of valuable contact time with the Internet material but often leads to classroom management and discipline problems. It is extremely important that teachers personally check the loading time of each site they select for the experience—not only the initial page but all of the links that students will visit as well. Teachers should download the sites using the same type of modem speed and, if at all possible, at the same time of day that the students will use the site. (Many connections download much slower during normal daily business hours than they do in the evening—the time when many teachers may be working on the field trip.)

Pages with graphics are always slower than pages with text: the more graphics, the slower the download time. Photographs take the longest time to download. Unless the page loads within sixty seconds, do not use it. Of course, there are exceptions to this rule, such as when those pages contain crucial information for the virtual field trip. Teachers need to determine whether to use a particular Internet link, while at the same time, determine a balance between the value of the page with the duration of the download time with the attention span of students.

A major consideration for this entire process is the modem speed of the computers that students are using. Computers on an ISDN or faster line or those with a 56K modem should have no problem with the downloading time of the vast majority of Internet sites. Modems with 36.6K and 28.8K usually do a sufficient job, unless there are a number of photographs posted. The problem becomes significant when dealing with modems of 14.4K or less. Those modems lead to considerable "dead time" while graphic-filled sites download. Still, in those situations where the students must deal with slow modem connections, teachers can do the following:

1. Bear with the long downloading time and give the students alternate assignments or activities within the study unit to work with while waiting for the graphics and photographs to download.
2. Discard all Internet sites that take over a minute to download; although, this might very well eliminate the majority of the collected sites.

3. Download Web sites ahead of time and load them into the computer's cache. A site loaded into the cache downloads very quickly once the students select it. The downside to this process is that teachers are limited to the number of sites due to the memory of the cache; although, there is usually sufficient memory for a small-scale virtual field trip. Each computer is different; teachers must discuss possibilities with the technology coordinator.

Luckily, companies rarely sell 14.4k modems anymore. Most new computers, even the bottom-of-the-line machines, such as the Internet-based iMac, are equipped with 56k modems. External 56k modems are also now available for under $100, which is a reasonable sum for most schools.

Reevaluate the Goals and Activities

A final decision that teachers need to make once they collect all the sites involves reevaluating the original goals, activities, and time frames that they proposed in the early stages of planning the activity. There are a number of basic but crucial questions teachers can ask. Teachers can reevaluate the initial plan, covering the following important areas:

Goals

1. Do the Internet sites still cover the original goals of the experience?
2. Are there new goals to add, based on unexpected material that was discovered?
3. Are there goals that are no longer appropriate or feasible based on the sites that were or were not found?

Activities

1. Are there sufficient URLs for students to visit for each activity that is planned? If not, is there time or desire to continue the search for additional sites, or should the proposed activity be dropped from the Internet session?
2. Do some of the sites suggest additional activities that should now be added to the virtual field trip?

Time Frame

1. Is the original anticipated time frame sufficient for using all of the selected Web sites?
2. Does the time frame need to be adjusted up or down?
3. Do sites need to be deleted or added in adjustment to the time scheduled for the online experience?

Curricular development is an evolving process. Remember that virtual field trips are but one part of an overall unit of study. It makes little sense to keep goals in the planning that, based on the curricular material available, are no longer achievable. Nor does it make sense to limit activities to the original goals, if new learning opportunities that logically fit within the curricular unit manifest themselves in the investigation for materials. If teachers take a holistic view of the virtual experience within the overall curricular unit, they can evaluate, adapt, plan, and coordinate goals and activities that provide the most substantial learning experience possible for students.

Make a Logical Plan to Implement into the Curriculum

After teachers adopt Internet sites, based on both their appropriateness and their connection with the original goals of the field trips, teachers can then make a logical plan for the implementation of the activities. This involves determining how students will conduct the virtual field trips, including the actual time limitations within the trips and the trips' places within the overall curricular units.

Create the trip structure

If teachers have not already decided, they need to ascertain how students will experience the virtual field trips. The various options include the following:

1. Conduct the trip together as an entire class, using one overhead-projected computer or a set of computers controlled by one central work station.

2. Let students conduct the trip on an individualized basis in a computer lab or at a classroom computer station where students can make their own decisions of which sites to visit and when to visit them.
3. Have students conduct the trip as an outside-the-classroom experience on a home, library, or community computer.

Teachers can combine any of these options, depending on the extent of their virtual field trips. In reality, this situation is no different than a real-life field trip. On an actual field trip to a museum, students usually receive an introduction as an entire group and view the most significant exhibit areas together. Then teachers presumably give them free time to investigate points of interest by themselves, with a partner, or in groups supervised by an adult. Finally, if students really enjoy the museum experience, they may choose to visit the museum again on their own time or with their families.

Teachers can set up virtual field trips in much the same fashion. Teachers can give students an introduction as a whole group, either with one computer connected to an overhead projector or by directing the students to visit particular Internet sites together as a group in a sequential fashion. Then students visit individual areas of interest at their personal computers on their own, with partners, or in groups. Finally, teachers can provide students with a list of URLs or a floppy disk containing either an outline or the html code for the field trip for use on a home computer.

Set time limits

Once teachers decide on all of these variables, they need to determine the time limitations for the miscellaneous aspects of the activities. Just as real field trips have certain limits on time, so do virtual field trips. Teachers need to answer the following:

- Which Internet sites are mandatory for all students to visit—either as a class or on an individualized basis?
- Which URLs are optional—those students choose based on their personal interests?

Again, these decisions vary based on the time frame of classes, the availability of the computers, and the specific curricular material teachers want to cover with the Internet experience.

SkyLight Professional Development

Provide URL Access

Once teachers decide on the structure of their trips, they need to plan how they will provide students with the URLs. There are various options, some very creative, some very straightforward. Teachers base these decisions on the amount of time they have available for this process. The following are some examples:

1. Create an itinerary for the trip. This is a list of stops students need to make, with or without time constraints. Teachers can design or outline the itinerary as a brochure, a pamphlet, or a custom-made stationary related to the subject matter of the trip.
2. Provide students with a comprehensive list of URLs to investigate, divided by subject matter.
3. Bookmark all of the potential sites on the classroom computer. (This is much more time consuming if teachers are using a computer lab.) Use different folders for various subject headings.
4. Create an original Web site, or a page on a school site, that takes students along the virtual field trip, link by link. (This is the scenario outlined in the original anecdote about the Boston Tea Party.) Create a map of the virtual location where the students can visually determine where they want to go next. This map can also serve as a home base for the trip experience.

Of course, there are many other possibilities. All it takes is an element of creativity on behalf of the teacher. The basic philosophy is to make the trip as exciting as possible to keep students' interest levels at an elevated state, while at the same time being cognizant of teacher-preparatory time limits.

Integrate Within the Curricular Unit

After teachers plan the trips, they need to place them within their overall curricular units. This is the key to valid, valuable curricular virtual field trips. The experience does not stand by itself, but it fits within an overall unit of study. In this regard, there are four basic areas that teachers need to determine and evaluate.

Learning Activities Before the Trip

1. What curricular areas do teachers need to cover before students embark on virtual field trips?
2. What prior knowledge do students need to ensure that they have the most productive educational experience possible?

Learning Activities After the Trip

1. What extensions of the trip can teachers initiate after the students conclude?
2. What curricular areas do teachers need to investigate based on the questions or problems raised by the experiences?
3. What assessment tools will teachers use to determine the amount of learning that results from virtual field trips?

Learning Activities Not Covered by the Trip

1. What curricular areas were *not* covered by the trip experience that need to be introduced using some other teaching methodology, be it through direct instruction, cooperative learning, or the use of classroom materials such as the textbook or other supplemental items?

Learning Activities Now Covered by the Trip

1. What unanticipated curricular areas were provided by the trip that now do *not* have to be covered or duplicated in other areas of the unit?

Check for Use of the Multiple Intelligences Theory

One of the most exciting new philosophies in educational theory is Gardner's (1993) multiple intelligences theory. This theory basically holds that everyone has a number of intelligences, some stronger than others. Each of them is brain based; that is, there is a precise location in the brain that directly controls that aspect of one's being. Intelligences include the following: visual/spatial, logical/ mathematical, verbal/linguistic, musical/rhythmic, bodily/kinesthetic, interpersonal, intrapersonal, and naturalist. By covering all of the intelligences in the curriculum, teachers ensure that every student has access to the material in the fashion that he or she best learns (Armstrong 1994).

With all curricula, teachers need to target multiple intelligences within the overall unit of study. Virtual field trips are ideal for addressing a number of intelligences. Therefore, virtual field trips automatically and easily lend themselves to the incorporation of the multiple intelligences theory.

Teachers can analyze the use of multiple intelligences once they conclude planning for the entire trip. It is a rather simple process for teachers to check if they are targeting all intelligences. All teachers need are copies of a multiple intelligences checklist and the basic plan for the overall curricular unit encompassing virtual field trips. Remember that the field trips are but one part of the entire curricular unit—each trip does not need to address every intelligence. (See The Natural Intelligence.)

The Civil War unit examined above, along with its Gettysburg virtual field trip, serves as an excellent example of this procedure (see Figure 3.5). Each of the intelligences is located within some aspect of the overall curricular material.

Once teachers complete the checklist, they can go back and fill in any holes. In the example above, after originally completing the Multiple Intelligences Checklist, Mr. Hughes immediately discovered that there was no plan for use of the musical intelligence. He went back to investigate a couple of the cultural-oriented URLs included within the trip plan. He soon found references to "Songs of the Civil War." Then he returned and included it as one of the listed visitation options for students. In addition, he downloaded and printed out some of the musical material with the intention of incor-

THE NATURALIST INTELLIGENCE

Recently, Gardner identified an eighth intelligence, the naturalist. However, there is very little classroom research on this new intelligence and virtually nothing outside the area of the sciences. For example, in a recent Educational Resources Information Center (ERIC) search of articles on multiple intelligences, out of 407 articles published, only two concerned the naturalist intelligence. The intelligence looks promising, but its practical application across the curriculum has yet to be determined.

Howard Gardner describes this intelligence as follows:

> Naturalist intelligence designates the human ability to discriminate among living things (plants, animals) as well as sensitivity to other features of the natural world (clouds, rock configurations). This ability was clearly of value in our evolutionary past as hunters, gatherers, and farmers; it continues to be central in such roles as botanist or chef. I also speculate that much of our consumer society exploits the naturalist intelligence, which can be mobilized in the discrimination among cars, sneakers, kinds of makeup, and the like. The kind of pattern recognition valued in certain of the sciences may also draw upon naturalist intelligence.
> (Checkley 1997, p. 8)

The naturalist intelligence is most applicable to the sciences. However, you can apply it to other curricular areas. Classifying and categorizing data are a few ways you can integrate this intelligence into other curricular areas.

Multiple Intelligences Checklist
Unit: The Civil War

INTELLIGENCE	CURRICULAR LOCATION
Verbal/Linguistic	Reading the book *Across Five Aprils*
Logical/Mathematical	The virtual field trip—exploring various items, manipulating data and materials
Visual/Spatial	The virtual field trip—viewing pictures and images
Bodily/Kinesthetic	Learning a folk dance introduced on a cultural site on the virtual field trip
Musical/Rhythmic	Learning a Civil War song discovered on the virtual field trip
Interpersonal	Cooperative group work within the unit
Intrapersonal	The virtual field trip—individual choices made during personal exploration time
Naturalist	Making a time line of Civil War events during the unit

Figure 3.5

porating it within the classroom after students concluded the trip, as a supplemental activity.

A multiple intelligences checklist can easily ensure that all of the intelligences are covered within the overall curricular unit. It also explicitly demonstrates how the virtual field trip is adding to the rich educational experiences of the students.

Address Assessment

How teachers address assessment is an individualized choice, wholly dependent on the particular virtual field trip experience and the overall curriculum. Unfortunately, in today's society, it seems as if teachers must determine all educational worth through quantitative means. In other words, if teachers cannot test or measure the material, it does not have value. This is an extremely unfortunate and ultimately frustrating position.

To assess a virtual field trip experience, teachers need to look back to the goals and parameters of the trip. If the virtual field trip is the major supplier of curricular information, then teachers can easily assess students on the end-of-unit evaluation. Teachers may want to provide worksheets asking specific questions about each site to ensure students cover the information. If the virtual field trip is solely meant to supplement material previously discussed, then teachers can informally assess students by having them reflect on the experience in journals or fill out a checklist or worksheet to verify that they visited some of the sites.

Virtual field trips are but one part of the overall curricular unit. The teacher instinctively knows if the experience is successful. If during the session students start going off-task and discipline problems arise after only a short period of computer time, chances are that there is a problem with the virtual field trip in that material for one reason or another is not keeping the students' attention. Then again, if all of the students are consistently on task, and there is significant complaining that they have to stop the activity when the period ends, then the teacher probably knows that the virtual field trip is a success. Teachers, act as "educational connoisseurs," determining the amount of learning going on during the trip and easily making value judgments about its worth. If confronted by administrators as to the end result of the online experience, teachers can use anecdotal examples describing the learning and enjoyment that students had during the virtual field trip (Eisner 1979).

In the example above, Mr. Hughes plans out his assessment ahead of time. He decides that the field trip is but one small part of his overall unit on the Civil War. Since there is already an adequate unit test that covers all the required material in the curriculum, he decides not to test students immediately after the experience.

Before the computer session, Mr. Hughes examines his original goals and determines that if the students visit all of the required sites, they will cover the material. However, he has a quandary that he himself experienced as he researched the trip—some of the sites are so interesting, students could spend hours at a single one. To ensure that the students visit all of the areas for at least a little while, he constructs the following short open-ended question assignment that students can complete while taking the trip:

SkyLight Professional Development

- Name at least one event that happened at the Battle of Gettysburg
- Name at least one type of food that people at that time ate
- Print out at least one verse of a song or poem of the Civil War
- Name at least one thing that a student your age might do during his or her free time during the Civil War years

If students answer all of these questions, Mr. Hughes knows that they visited most of the locations. The questions are short and easy enough that they will not keep students at one link, preventing them from spending time at areas of greater interest. Students can then share their answers in a classroom discussion as they debrief after the virtual field trip experience.

As Mr. Hughes' students take the virtual field trip, he observes closely. For one of the few times all year, all of his students are on task throughout the entire learning experience. In fact, they are rather upset and demand additional time when the virtual field trip is over. As final proof of the learning that took place, students continue to offer material they acquired from the trip throughout classroom discussions for the next month. Mr. Hughes concludes that his students acquired a tremendous amount of knowledge, rendering the virtual field trip experience a resounding success.

A Virtual Field Trip Checklist

The following is a summary of the various aspects involved in creating virtual field trips, covering all of the various areas previously discussed. A full-scale version of this information in the form of a blank checklist, suitable for the reproduction, appears in appendix A.

When planning for an extensive online learning experience such as a virtual field trip, the first task that teachers must do is determine goals and parameters. In particular, teachers need to ask the following questions:

- *Why* am I planning this specific trip?
- *What* curricular material will this trip cover?
- *How* will this experience enhance the students' learning in this unit?

The next step that teachers need to take is to brainstorm ideas for the options that students will investigate on the trip. The easiest and most efficient tool is a webbing worksheet, in which teachers can lay out all of the goals and connecting activities with the paths that students would take clearly visible.

Once teachers define the activities for their trips, they can then investigate Internet sites to search for URLs that students can visit. This is the most time-consuming aspect of planning virtual field trips; although, the time required is wholly dependent on the generality of the topic: the more general the topic, the easier it is to locate materials. The process of securing Internet sites that teachers want to include involves using search engines and directories, general educational sites, subject-matter sites, and teacher guest books. Another important consideration is the individual teacher's experience. The more comfortable teachers are with locating material on the Internet, the less time they need for the search.

Finally, after teachers complete all of the ground work, there are a number of important decisions that teachers must make. First, they must analyze the appropriateness of the sites they collect. Then they need to reevaluate the goals and activities of the virtual field trips to determine if anything has changed based on the Web sites that are available. Teachers must then design logical plans to implement the Web sites into the overall curriculum, taking care to determine what activities need to go before and after the online experience. When teachers conclude all other planning, they need to make sure the trips target multiple intelligences to ensure that every student is exposed to every intelligence at some point in the overall curricular unit.

The next chapter provides a step-by-step example of this process of creating a virtual field trip, following the procedure outlined in this chapter. It demonstrates the vast potential of virtual field trips for the enhancement of the curriculum, while simultaneously exhibiting the ease with which classroom teachers can create a valid, interesting, and useful curricular experience for their students.

CREATING A VIRTUAL FIELD TRIP FROM START TO FINISH

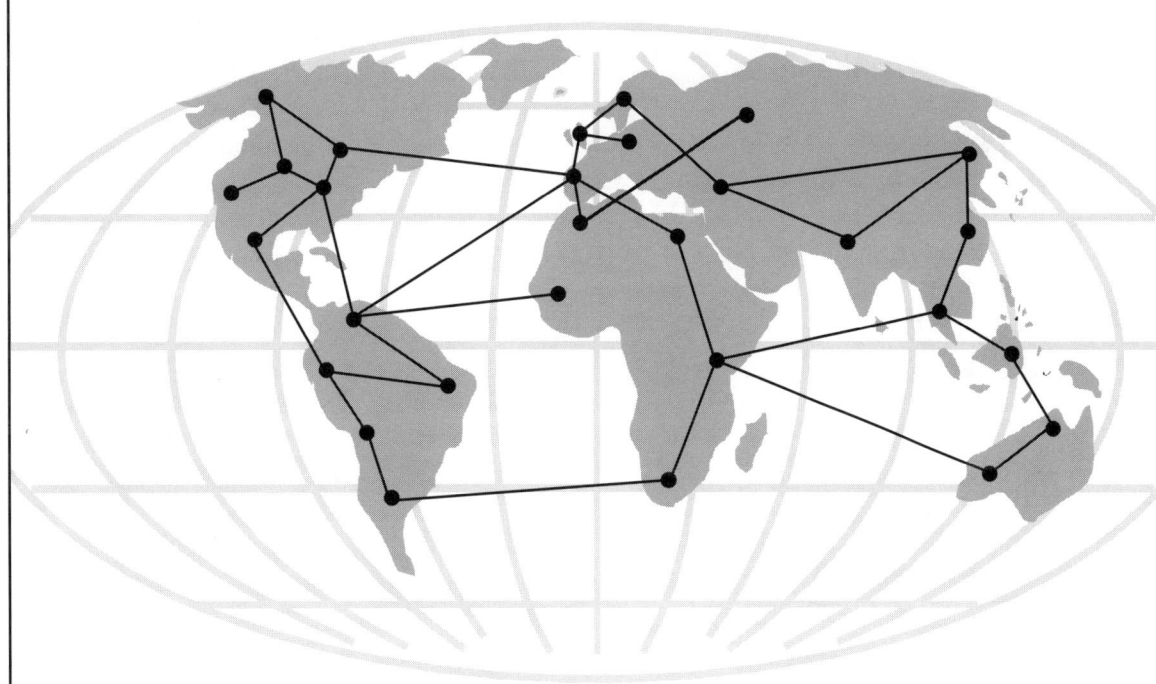

CHAPTER FOUR

Creating a Virtual Field Trip from Start to Finish

CHAPTER 4

Here Presenteth Thy Dilemma

Ms. Gifford* faces a classroom dilemma. Actually, it is a language arts teacher's nightmare. Her curriculum for ninth grade demands that students read the play *Romeo and Juliet* and learn about William Shakespeare—his life and times. Unfortunately, her students found an introductory excerpt of this particular play to be exceedingly boring, and they had absolutely no interest whatsoever in the study of his life. She showed them the movie *Romeo and Juliet*, but her students were not overly impressed by the dramatization of the story nor of the visual cultural background that the film provided. She even considered showing the most recent movie version in which the story is played out in modern times, using gang rivalries as the basis of the storyline. However, she discarded that idea. Even though that version presented the basic story in Shakespearean dialect, it made "true" Shakespeare seem even more out of touch with these students' interests. At least that was the opinion of those students who had already viewed that particular movie.

*All names of teachers are fictional.

Ms. Gifford instinctively knows that she has to do something innovative to capture student interest in this curricular area. Standardized testing at the end of the year covers this material, and their tenth grade language arts curriculum builds on it with the play *Julius Caesar*. Like it or not, her students need to learn the material and not just read the play.

Looking at her long-term schedule she notices that she is scheduled for a couple of hours in the school computer lab within the next two weeks. Ms. Gifford is aware that her students love to get onto the Internet regardless of the reason. Even research papers are not dreaded as much when she allows students to incorporate research from the Internet. She comes up with a brainstorm: Using her time in the computer lab, she can create a virtual field trip for her students in which they can travel back in time to the era of William Shakespeare.

. . . .

Putting the Methodology to Work

This chapter provides teachers with a practical example of how to create a personal virtual field trip for their students. The example follows the exact methodology outlined in the previous chapter. Ms. Gifford* walks through the entire process of planning, researching, creating, and implementing her own curricular-based virtual field trip. She demonstrates all of her decisions and legwork, along with each Internet site she visits, so that teachers of all Internet-comfort levels can easily follow her step-by-step process on their own computer with their own Internet connection.

Most important, teachers can look at this chapter as an example of how anyone, in any subject, in any grade, can construct his or her own virtual field trip. Teachers can adapt all of the steps to their own curricula. This particular example uses subject matter that is well known to the vast majority of teachers. Although this example is set in high school, even

---

*All names of teachers are fictional.

early elementary teachers can use this process to develop an experience for younger students.

In this chapter only, URLs are added to Web site descriptions. This helps teachers to follow easily the process outlined in this exercise. For all other sites mentioned throughout this book, please continue to look in appendix C to find the appropriate URL. Be aware that some of the listed URLs may no longer be functional, while new and better sites may become apparent. Either way, having slightly differing examples should in no way impede the understanding of the process involved with the creation of a personal virtual field trip.

Determining Goals and Parameters

The first step that Ms. Gifford needs to accomplish is to determine the various goals and parameters for this activity. She asks herself the three basic goal-oriented questions:
- *Why* am I planning this specific trip?
- *What* curricular material will this trip cover?
- *How* will this experience enhance the students' learning in this unit?

For the first question, "*Why* am I planning this specific trip?" Ms. Gifford decides that this virtual field trip experience will have the following goals:

Goal #1: At the end of the activity, students will be able to analyze, synthesize, and evaluate various historical and cultural aspects and components of the Shakespearean era and to explain how Shakespeare's work was influenced by these factors.

Goal #2: At the end of the activity, students will have a better appreciation of the culture surrounding both Shakespeare and his work.

Based on the district curricular standards that provide the basic outline for this particular language arts class, Ms. Gifford considers the second question, "*What* curricular material will this trip cover?" She decides that the trip will cover the following curricular material:
- The life Shakespeare probably experienced
- Information about where and how his various plays were performed

- Elizabethan culture (dress, activities, way of life)
- Political climate of that period

For the third question, "*How* will this experience enhance the students' learning in this unit?" Ms. Gifford considers what this activity will provide that other methodologies will not. Basically, she needs to answer how this experience will enhance students' learning in this unit. Otherwise, the activity will ultimately prove to be a waste of time. She decides that the experience will enhance student learning, based on the following:

1. The activity will give students visual examples of the various aspects and components of Shakespearean-era England.
2. The activity will allow students to pursue personal areas of interest with the study.
3. Based on the students' previous affinity for online activities, they will most likely be more engaged and more on task with the curricular material; therefore, a higher level of learning will take place over using other materials and methodologies.

Now that Ms. Gifford has answered these three basic questions, she next determines the scope of the actual virtual field trip. She considers how much of the unit she will cover in this particular learning activity. She decides that the trip will cover the following aspects:

- The daily life of William Shakespeare's era
- The culture of the time
- Limited background of the political nature of the period

Ms. Gifford determines that the trip will be the major source of curricular information in the first two areas and will reinforce discussions her students have already had concerning the political atmosphere of the period.

The last area Ms. Gifford needs to decide on is the type of student assessment she will use. Ms. Gifford decides that students will create booths (posters and displays) of some item of the Shakespearean era. The booths will demonstrate their analysis, synthesis, and evaluation of the curricular material. The information that they find on the Internet will serve as the basis for this project.

SkyLight Professional Development

Creating a Virtual Field Trip from Start to Finish

Brainstorming for Shakespeare

Next Ms. Gifford brainstorms ideas for this virtual field trip. She wants to organize all her initial ideas so she can easily check them for viability and practicality.

She decides to use a web of possibilities graphic organizer. She maps out ideas using the decisions she made about goals and parameters (see Figure 4.1).

Original Web of Possibilities for the "Shakespeare: His Life and Times" Virtual Field Trip

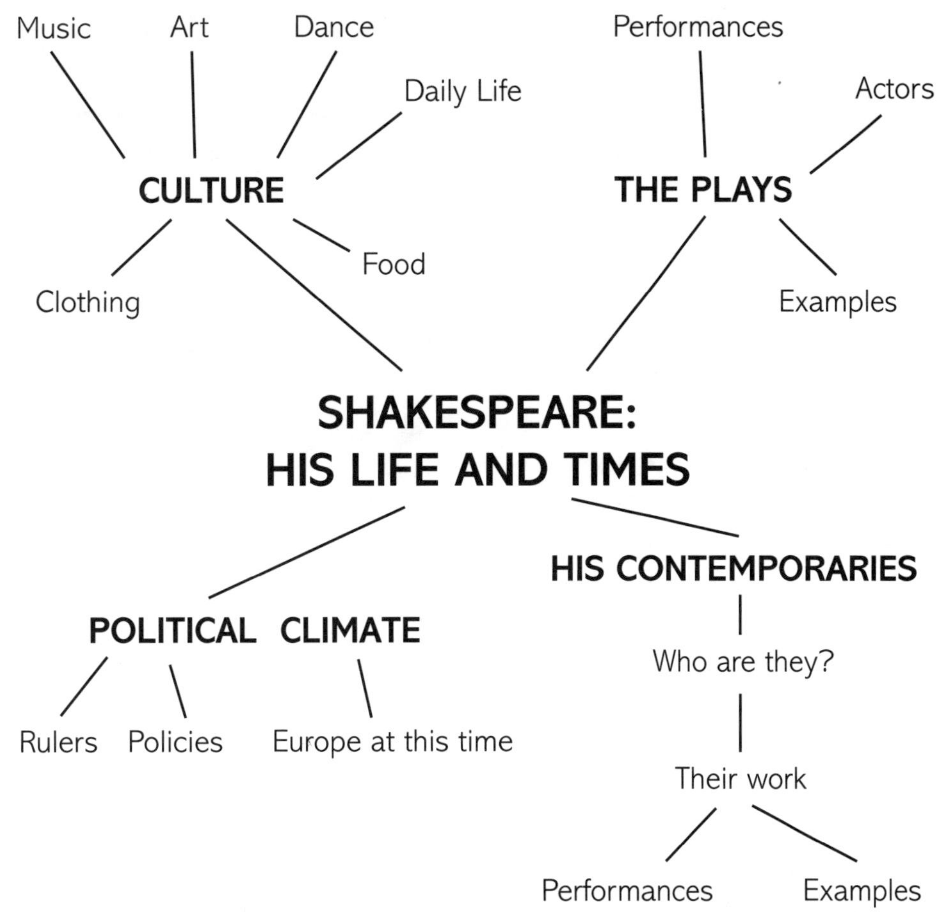

- CULTURE: Music, Art, Dance, Daily Life, Food, Clothing
- THE PLAYS: Performances, Actors, Examples
- SHAKESPEARE: HIS LIFE AND TIMES
- POLITICAL CLIMATE: Rulers, Policies, Europe at this time
- HIS CONTEMPORARIES: Who are they?, Their work (Performances, Examples)

Figure 4.1

After completing the web, Ms. Gifford then analyzes each of the various ideas to determine their viability. First, she needs to ensure that each idea truly matches one of the original curricular goals. She quickly constructs an impromptu table to assist her in determining this correlation (see Figure 4.2).

Checking the Viability of Ideas on the Web of Possibilities		
BASIC AREA	**CONNECTED AREAS**	**GOAL IT MATCHES**
CULTURE	Music, art, dance, dailylife, food, clothing	#1—Analyze, synthesize, evaluate aspects/components of era/his work #2—Appreciation of culture
THE PLAYS	Performances, actors, examples	#1—Analyze, synthesize, evaluate aspects/components of era/his work
POLITICAL CLIMATE	Rulers, policies, Europe at this time	#1—Analyze, synthesize, evaluate aspects/components of era/his work
HIS CONTEMPORARIES	Who are they? Their work: performances & examples	#1—Analyze, synthesize, evaluate aspects/components of era/his work #2—Appreciation of culture

Figure 4.2

From the table, Ms. Gifford determines that she can match each of these proposed connected areas, or activities as she considers them, to her original curricular goals. Now she needs to check for the practicality of the activities. To determine practicality, Ms. Gifford needs to take into account the classroom or lab time available for the virtual field trip, the age and abilities of the students, and the material resources at hand. She considers her specific situation as she works through each of the variables:

Lab Time Available: Only two days. If her class meets her at the lab, if she has the virtual field trip already downloaded onto the computers and operational, and if she saves opening business time activities, the students will have approximately ninety minutes of actual working time on the Internet.

Age and Abilities of Students: These are high school students who are already Internet savvy. They do not need an introduction of how to work online. They are basically an average class as far as reading level is concerned, so they should not have any significant problems with the reading levels found on the vast majority of the Web sites.

Material Resources at Hand: Still unknown, although through her preliminary checks, she determines that there is sufficient material online to cover the areas she proposes to study.

The first of these three areas, lab time available, immediately concerns Ms. Gifford. Ninety minutes is a highly limited time frame to work with, even if she prepares students ahead of time to maximize their efforts. She needs to decide if she wants her students to have a broad introductory experience covering all of the topics or if she should narrow them down so that students only delve deeper into a few. Again, her goals to have students analyze, synthesize, and evaluate along with appreciate the material sway her to cut down the list of investigative topics. Subsequently, she ranks and evaluates her four original areas of activity:

Culture
- Very important
- The main reason for doing the activity

The Plays
- Also very important
- The subareas of performances and actors are significantly more important than spending time on textual examples
- Since students will read *Romeo and Juliet* along with some other supplemental materials in class, textual examples can be removed

Political Climate
- Somewhat important, although on a small basis
- Much of this material is covered in other curricular areas
- The section on Europe at this Time can definitely be removed
- Need to see what is available online before making a final determination about rulers and policies

VIRTUAL FIELD TRIPS IN THE CYBERAGE

Contemporaries
- Not important
- Some of this material is covered in other areas of the curriculum
- This whole section can be removed

Once Ms. Gifford eliminates impractical areas, she rewrites the original web, this time including only those planned stops for the virtual field trip experience. In this version, she leaves room to add titles and URLs that she might find for each of the areas (see Figure 4.3).

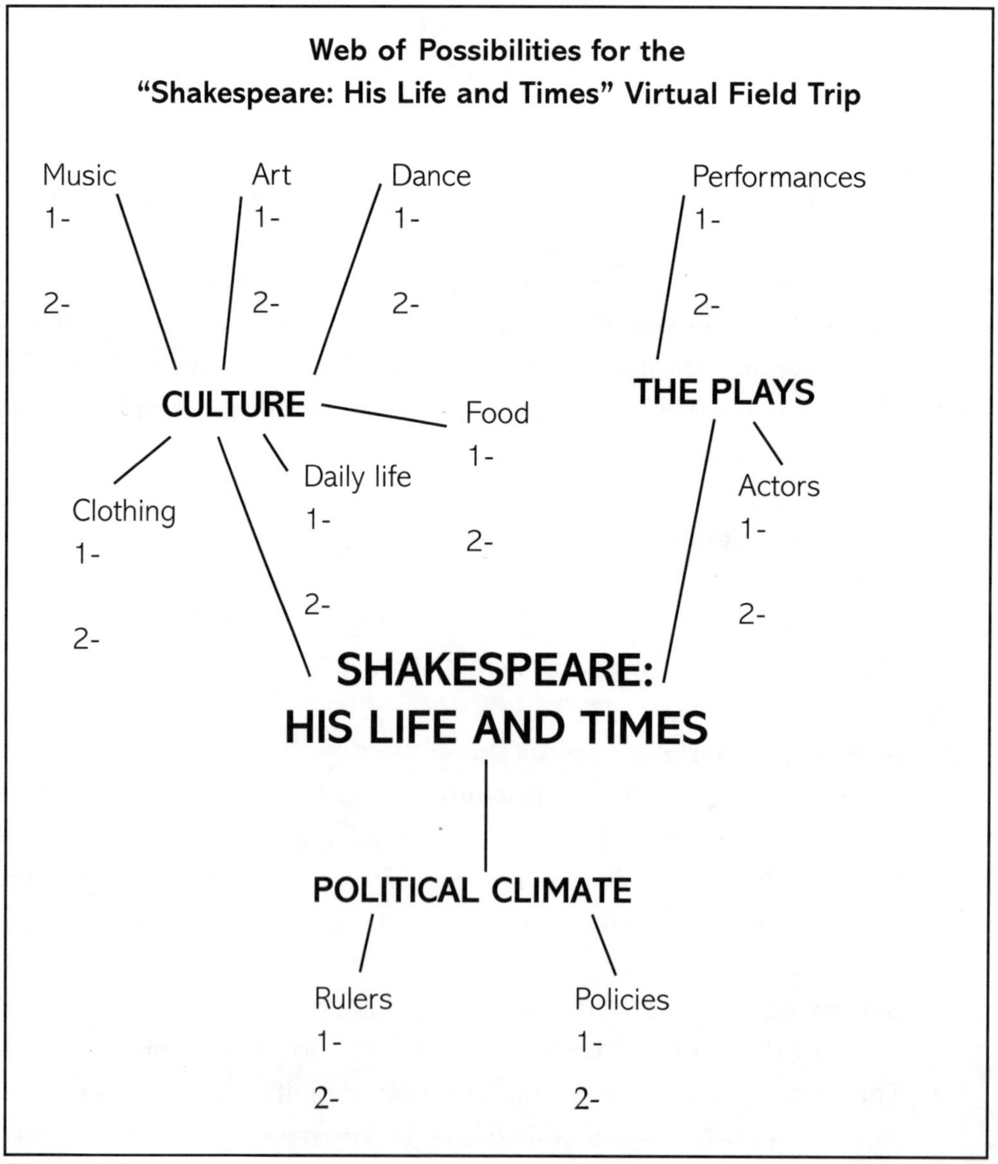

**Web of Possibilities for the
"Shakespeare: His Life and Times" Virtual Field Trip**

Music
1-
2-

Art
1-
2-

Dance
1-
2-

Performances
1-
2-

CULTURE — Food
1-
2-

THE PLAYS

Clothing
1-
2-

Daily life
1-
2-

Actors
1-
2-

**SHAKESPEARE:
HIS LIFE AND TIMES**

POLITICAL CLIMATE

Rulers
1-
2-

Policies
1-
2-

Figure 4.3

SkyLight Professional Development

Now that Ms. Gifford has a working plan of areas to cover on her virtual field trip experience, the next step is to begin investigating the possible Internet sites to include in her virtual field trip.

Linking to Shakespeare

Ms. Gifford knows that a number of sites dealing with the topic of Shakespeare exist on the Internet, but she is not quite sure how many. She quickly does a search for the term Shakespeare, using INFOSEEK. To her astonishment, she discovers exactly 351,998 different links to Web sites containing that particular term. Obviously, she does not have the time to sort through such a ridiculous number. She tries using the search engine METACRAWLER, which she knows will limit her search to the top ten sites from each of the major search engines (see chapter 2).

Using the same search term on METACRAWLER, Ms. Gifford retrieves fifty-six of the top sites in the various search engine databases. Even a full investigation of only those fifty-six sites will still take a number of hours. Therefore, while scrolling through the list and reading each of the descriptions, she decides to limit her initial investigation to only specific types of sites. Her criteria is as follows:

1. Include sites that appear as if they are of a general nature about Shakespeare, especially if they mention experiential activities or state that they include additional resources, especially further Internet links.
2. Include sites that look as if they cover unique topics, such as the Globe Theater, discussions of Victorian ethics or anti-Semitism, or some other specialized, interesting item appropriate to this time period.
3. Do *not* include sites that state that they contain Shakespearean texts (having already made the decision not to include those in the virtual field trip).
4. Do *not* include sites that look as if they contain scholarly research papers.

Ms. Gifford pares down the list to a more manageable dozen. The following sites are from Ms. Gifford's list, presented with the complete text

SkyLight Professional Development

and descriptions as she sees them on her computer screen, minus duplicated entries and descriptions:

Shakespeare Web
Excite: Here's a fish hangs in the net like a poor man's right in the law. 'Twill hardly come out. Welcome to the Shakespeare Web . . . an interactive, hypermedia environment dedicated to the increasingly popular understanding and enjoyment of Shakespeare's plays and other works. nbsp;
Infoseek: Interactive page with Queries & Replies, answers to common questions and information about troupes, festivals and performances.
http://www.shakespeare.com/ (Excite, Infoseek, WebCrawler)

Shakespeare Magazine
Excite, WebCrawler: A convergence of in-depth and up-to-the-minute information from Shakespeare scholars, teachers, and theatre professionals.
Thunderstone: Welcome to the premiere Shakespeare teaching resource site on the Internet. Inside the Shakespeare magazine vault you will uncover a wealth of lessons created by our editors, and gathered from popular teaching resources.
http://www.shakespearemag.com/ (Excite, Thunderstone, WebCrawler, Yahoo!)

Internet Shakespeare resources
Excite, WebCrawler: I don't guarantee the completeness of this list. I update it as I have time, and as I discover interesting new sites. (I also don't purport to have a listing of all classes or festivals—only those available on the Web.)
http://the-tech.mit.edu/Shakespeare/other.html (Excite, WebCrawler)

Shakespeare in Love
http://movies.yahoo.com/movies...guide/shakespeare_in_love.html (Yahoo!)

Shakespeare page
Hey, Nonnie Nonnie! Yond webpage moveth! Update thy bookmarks to:
http://daphne.palomar.edu/shakespeare/Home.
http://www.palomar.edu/Library/shake.htm (AltaVista)

The Folger Shakespeare Library
Excite: The Folger Shakespeare Library® is an independent research library. Opened in 1932, the Folger was a gift to the American people from Henry Clay Folger and his wife Emily Jordan Folger. A major center for scholarly research, the Folger houses the world's largest collection of Shakespeare's printed works, in addition to a magnificent collection of other rare Renaissance books and . . .
http://www.folger.edu/welcome.htm (AltaVista, Excite)

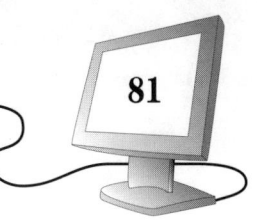

Mr. William Shakespeare and the Internet
http://daphne.palomar.edu/shakespeare/ (Infoseek)
Pages at this site with the same name:
http://daphne.palomar.edu/Shakespeare/

Shakespeare - Globe
Festival im Globe Neuss 2. Juni bis 25. SHAKESPEARE e-mail: <webmaster@widd.de> Willkommen im Globe Neuss, einem Nachbau des Shakespear´schen Globe Theaters, in dem jedes Jahr das Shakespeare-Festival stattfindet.
http://www.widd.de/shakespeare.globe/ (WebCrawler)

Shakespeare and Anti-Semitism: The Question of Shylock
- analysis of Elizabethan anti-semitism in Shakespeare's "The Merchant of Venice" and the character of Shylock.
http://www.geocities.com/Athens/Acropolis/7221/ (Yahoo!)

Audio Recordings of Shakespeare
Sonnets read by Sir John Gielgud. Excerpts from "Much Ado About Nothing" with Rex Harrison and Rachel Roberts, and "Julius Caesar" with Ralph Richardson and Anthony Quayle.
http://town.hall.org/Archives/...rperAudio/020994_harp_ITH.html (Infoseek)

The Rebuilding of Shakespeare's Globe Theatre
http://www.clock.co.uk/face/features/0895/index.30.1.html (AltaVista)

Shakespeare's Globe
Shakespeare's Globe rebuilt in London
http://www.rdg.ac.uk/globe/Globe.html (Infoseek)

Ms. Gifford can copy and save this list into a word processing document. As she works with the sites, she can cut and paste the individual URLs into her browser, saving her considerable time (not having to type in the individual URLs) and frustration later on (not having to run repeated METACRAWLER searches).

Now that she has a list of potential Internet sites, Ms. Gifford can construct a simple chart to use as she analyzes these Web pages. By recording her analysis, she can easily keep track of which sites are worthwhile to include. She also can tell if there are holes in her research—areas that she wants to include that this particular search does not cover. The chart includes all of the subtopic areas from her web of possibilities along the top, and the Internet sites she chose listed along the side (see Figure 4.4).

VIRTUAL FIELD TRIPS IN THE CYBERAGE

Analysis of Web Sites Located on METACRAWLER

WEB SITE	CULTURE						PLAYS		POLITICS	
	Art	Clo	Dan	DL	Fd	Mus	Actr	Perf	Rlrs	Pol
Shakespeare Web										
NOTES: empty										
Shakespeare Magazine										
NOTES: paid subscriptions only										
Internet Shks Resources										
NOTES: no useful links										
Shakespeare in Love										
NOTES: just a movie review										
Shakespeare Page										
NOTES: old link to Mr. W. Shks site										
Folger Shakespeare Lib										
NOTES: useless										
Mr. W. Shks and the Int.	X?	X?	X?	X?	X?	X?			XX	
NOTES: GREAT! timeline—life/times; links to Renaissance stuff										
Shakespeare Globe										
NOTES: in German—useless										
Shks & Anti-Semitism										
NOTES: too advanced										
Audio Recordings										
NOTES: too long to download; no R & J recordings										
Rebuilding of Globe Thtr								X		
NOTES: not as good as Sh. Globe site										
Shakespeare's Globe				X			XX	XX		
NOTES: GREAT! virtual tour of Globe; many links; picts of med Lon										

KEY:
Art = Arts   Fd = Food   Perf = Performances
Clo = Clothing   Mus = Music   Rlrs = Rulers
Dan = Dance   Actr = Actors   Pol = Policies
DL = Daily life

Figure 4.4

Creating a Virtual Field Trip from Start to Finish

Out of the twelve sites that Ms. Gifford analyzes, she finds only two of them to be really useful. The sites she selects cover both the plays and the politics sections of the virtual field trip. Before she spends additional time following link to link on those sites to locate curricular material on culture, she decides to investigate some educational sites—sites that may not be listed on the general consumer search engines.

Ms. Gifford knows that the easiest way to discover educational-oriented subject-matter sites is to start with a general educational site and see what sites it recommends. Therefore, she decides to first try KATHY SCHROCK'S GUIDE FOR EDUCATORS. Under the listing "Subject Access" she tries the link marked "Literature/Language Arts." On that page, she finds the following potentially useful site:

Medieval English Literature (1350-1485)
. . . an online anthology of links and information dealing with Medieval English authors and their works (http://www.luminarium.org/medlit).

Unfortunately, upon careful examination, she discovers that this link led to the same Mr. William Shakespeare site that proved so useful in the METACRAWLER search.

Considering that she is missing material on culture, Ms. Gifford decides to look at the "History and Social Studies" category on the general educational Web site. On that page there are three categories: American History Resources, World History Resources, and General History and Social Studies Sites. She decides to try the link to "World History Sites." On that page, she notices one potentially useful site:

Castles on the Web
. . . a beautiful site which links the castle resources on the Internet including history and photographs. (http://www.castlesontheweb.com)

Although this is a category she did not originally anticipate, the material is appropriate to her virtual field trip. Therefore, for the time being, she adds the site to her chart of useful Web sites.

Switching over to the "General History and Social Studies Sites" category, she finds the following links:

History/Social Studies for K-12 Teachers
. . . a well-arranged site which includes extensive, annotated links to help social studies teachers find information on the Internet. (http://www.execpc.com/~dboals/boals.html)

SkyLight Professional Development

History of Costume
... an online reproduction of a 1880's book that provides drawings of historical dress from antiquity to the end of the 19th century. (http://www.siue.edu/COSTUMES/TEXT_INDEX.HTML)

The HISTORY/SOCIAL STUDIES FOR K-12 TEACHERS site has numerous categories to choose from, each containing hundreds of additional subject-matter Web sites. Before she goes exploring along this road, she decides to first check out the History of Costume site. There she discovers paintings of typical clothes of Shakespearean England; therefore, she adds this site to her chart of useful Web sites.

Returning to the HISTORY/SOCIAL STUDIES FOR K–12 TEACHERS site, Ms. Gifford selects the category marked "European History Sources," which provides her with 200 sources. Among them are the following potentially useful links and descriptions:

LBMS—The Middle Ages
Created by 7th grade students to teach about Life in the Middle Ages. (http://schools.ci.burbank.ca.us/~luther/midages/beginhere.html)

Exhibits Collection—The Middle Ages
Remember the programs from The Western Tradition? This exhibit replicates some aspects of the video series of the Annenberg/CPB Multimedia Collection. (http://www.learner.org/exhibits/middleages)

Medieval and Renaissance Instruments
An amazing collection of research on musical instruments, with some traced back to ancient Sumeria (bagpipe). All or most of the pages provide a text summary of the history of the instrument and links to other research (print mainly) resources. The page also provides graphics.
(http://www.s-hamilton.k12.ia.us/antiqua/instrumt.html)

Wharram: a look at peasants in the Middle Ages
Ever wonder what life must have been like for peasants in the Middle Ages? (http://loki.stockton.edu/~ken/wharram/wharram.htm)

Wichamstow—a virtual Medieval village
Find out about life in a Medieval Village. This site lets you wander. (http://www.ftech.net/~regia/estate.htm)

Medieval/Renaissance Food Homepage
(http://www.pbm.com/~lindahl/food.html)

SkyLight Professional Development

Medieval Art and Architecture
Vast and detailed. Thumbnails and full multi-page graphics of structures in England and France. More European nations scheduled for the future. (http://vrlab.fa.pitt.edu/medart/menuengl/maineng.html)

Ms. Gifford then adds these sites to her previous chart of Web site analyses (see Figure 4.5).

Supplemental Analysis of Web Sites Located Through General Educational Sites										
	CULTURE						PLAYS		POLITICS	
WEB SITE	Art	Clo	Dan	DL	Fd	Mus	Actr	Perf	Rlrs	Pol
Castles on the Web				X					X	
NOTES:	unexpected site—virtual tours of medieval castles									
LBMS - The Middle Ages	XX	XX	XX	XX	XX	XX				
NOTES:	GREAT! only drawback—it's made by mid sch students									
Exhibits Collection	XX	XX	XX	XX	XX	XX				
NOTES:	GREAT! all aspects of culture; activity based									
Med & Ren Instruments						XX				
NOTES:	GREAT! original picts with costume and sounds									
Wharram				XX						
NOTES:	GREAT! tour of lost medieval peasant village									
Wichamstow				XX						
NOTES:	GREAT! virtual medieval village									
Med/Ren Food Page						XX				
NOTES:	GREAT! dozens of articles and info about med food									
Med Art and Architecture	XX									
NOTES:	GREAT! lots of photos—student controlled									

KEY:
Art = Arts
Clo = Clothing
Dan = Dance
DL = Daily life
Fd = Food
Mus = Music
Actr = Actors
Perf = Performances
Rlrs = Rulers
Pol = Policies

Figure 4.5

After this search of educational Internet sites, Ms. Gifford decides that she has enough material to put together her two-day virtual field trip. Still, as one last easy search for information, she decides to post the following message on the teacher guest book of the general education site TEACHERS HELPING TEACHERS. She hopes that a teacher will suggest a site that she possibly missed somewhere:

I am constructing a virtual field trip on the Internet for students to experience the life and times of William Shakespeare. Does anyone have any suggestions? I'm mostly looking for sites on the culture of the time, not textual material. Thanks!

Within twenty-four hours, Ms. Gifford receives four messages, including the following suggestions (the cities are added for identification purposes):

I've used http://198.50.0.166/shakes.htm. It's a good site for basic information. You also might try searching for Elizabethan England. BOSTON

Here are a couple of sites from dogpile.com that look promising:
Mr. Shakespeare at http://daphne.palomar.edu/shakespeare/sitemap.htm
Shakespeare Links on the Internet at http://www.shakespeare-oxford.com/shaklink.htm SAN FRANCISCO

I've used the search engine at: http://www.whatuseek.com/cgi-bin/redirect.go?url=http://www.legends.dm.net/shakespeare/
Also, look at The Life and Times of William Shakespeare at http://www.stratford.co.uk/hislife/ TORONTO

I've used Shakespeare the Man: His Life and Times:
http://members.tripod.com/~JeanneAnn/shakebio.htm
This is cool - A Shakespearean Quest—a research-type game: http://www.sinc.sunysb.edu/Stu/ldimiche/webshak.htm
This is similar to the above, but maybe a little more detailed:
http://islander.phs.poquoson.k12.va.us/public/DUBOSE.HTM CLEVELAND

Ms. Gifford investigates each of these sites. A number of the pages are sites that she already evaluated; however, two of them are quite interesting and potentially usable, so she adds them to her table of sites (see Figure 4.6).

SkyLight Professional Development

Supplemental Analysis of Web Sites Located Through Guest Book Responses										
	CULTURE						PLAYS		POLITICS	
WEB SITE	Art	Clo	Dan	DL	Fd	Mus	Actr	Perf	Rlrs	Pol
Life and Times of W. S.							X?	X?		
NOTES:	GREAT! material on the man—quick and easy									
Shks the Man: Lif & Tms							X?	X?		
NOTES:	good—but not as good as previous one									

KEY:
Art = Arts   Fd = Food   Perf = Performances
Clo = Clothing   Mus = Music   Rlrs = Rulers
Dan = Dance   Actr = Actors   Pol = Policies
DL = Daily life

Figure 4.6

To conclude her search, Ms. Gifford does a quick survey of her completed table. She determines that there is at least one usable Web site for each category. Overall, she now has twelve potential sites to include in the virtual field trip. Now comes the important step: deciding which sites to actively use and how to use them.

Making the Final Decisions

Before she makes any final decisions, Ms. Gifford first completes her web of possibilities, placing each of the twelve selected sites in their appropriate locations (see Figure 4.7).

Analyzing the Appropriateness of the Shakespeare Sites

The next important task Ms. Gifford performs is an analysis of the sites that she collected. She already conducted a quick preliminary analysis of the pages as she first discovered them, immediately eliminating those that she

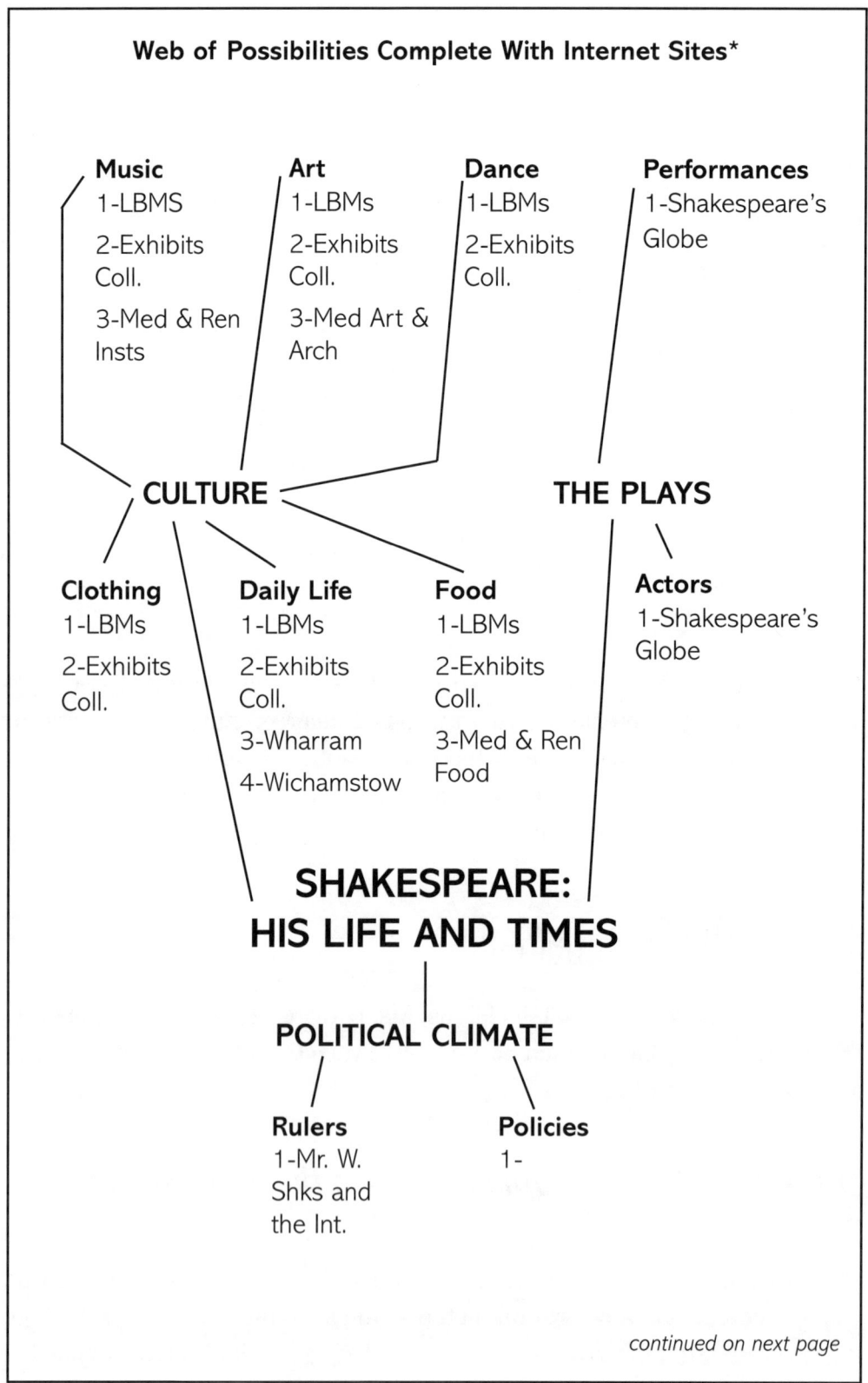

Figure 4.7

Creating a Virtual Field Trip from Start to Finish

TITLES & URL'S*

Exhibits Collection (learner.org/exhibits/middleages)
LBMS - The Middle Ages
   (schools.ci.burbank.ca.us/~luther/midages/beginhere.html)
Medieval Art and Architecture
   (vrlab.fa.pitt.edu/medart/menuengl/maineng.html)
Medieval & Renaissance Food Page
   (pbm.com/~lindahl/food.html)
Medieval & Renaissance Instruments
   (s-hamilton.k12.ia.us/antiqua/instrumt.html)
Mr. William Shakespeare and the Internet
   (daphne.palomar.edu/shakespeare)
Shakespeare's Globe
   (rdg.ac.uk/globe/Globe.html)
Wharram
   (loki.stockton.edu/~ken/wharram/wharram.htm)
Wichamstow
   (ftech.net/~regia/estate.htm)

**INTERNET SITES NOT INCLUDED ON WEB
FOR LACK OF APPROPRIATE LOCATION***

Castles on the Web
   (castlesontheweb.com)
Life and Times of William Shakespeare
   (stratford.co.uk/hislife)
Shakespeare the Man: Life and Times
   (members.tripod.com/~JeanneAnn/shakebio.htm)

*For the sake of space, the "http://www." of all URLs on the web of possibilities has been excluded.

Figure 4.7 continued

instantly knew were not appropriate for her needs. Now she needs to conduct a more detailed analysis to ensure that the material she selects is both age-appropriate for her high school students and that the site itself downloads within a reasonable amount of time. She has as many as three or four appropriate sites for many of the categories, so she also assumes that this analysis might eliminate a couple of the duplicate sites.

SkyLight Professional Development

For her criteria, Ms. Gifford decides that she will only use Internet pages written at the high school level unless, of course, a site is the only one available for a particular category. She will make an exception only if the site contains excellent graphics or virtual information that will significantly enhance the trip. She also decides that unless a site downloads within a minute, using the 56K modems that her computer lab has, she will not use it on the virtual field trip. Having the students wait more than a minute of download time could lead to off-task behavior, besides being a significant waste of lab time for only a two-day excursion.

Using the twelve sites that she already selected, Ms. Gifford makes a quick chart to conduct her analysis (see Figure 4.8).

Analysis of Reading Levels and Download Times		
INTERNET SITE NAME	READING LEVEL	DOWNLOAD TIME (56K)
Exhibits Collection	OK	17 seconds
LBMS - The Middle Ages	young—7th gd	11 seconds
Medieval Art and Architecture	OK	32 seconds
Medieval & Renaissance Food Page	OK	7 seconds
Medieval & Renaissance Instruments	OK	11 seconds
Mr. W. Shakespeare & the Internet	OK	28 seconds
Shakespeare's Globe	OK	21 seconds
Wharram	OK	12 seconds
Wichamstow	OK	11 seconds
Castles on the Web	OK	26 seconds
Life & Times of William Shakespeare	OK	16 seconds
Shakespeare the Man: Life and Times	OK	87 seconds

Figure 4.8

Creating a Virtual Field Trip from Start to Finish

While examining her data and simultaneously comparing it to her last version of the web of possibilities (see Figure 4.7), she determines that she can easily eliminate two potentially problematic Internet sites:

1. LBMS - The Middle Ages site has a reading level below her students' abilities. This site will not impact the trip since she has alternate sites in every area.
2. Shakespeare the Man: Life and Times site took over a minute to download. This too will not impact the trip since the category is not yet on the web and she has an alternate site that covers the same basic material.

Ms. Gifford now has ten sites to incorporate into her virtual field trip. Now she has to compare these activities with the original goals and activities she planned for the virtual field trip experience.

Reevaluating the Goals and Activities

Ms. Gifford gathers her list of goals and her latest version of her web of possibilities to conduct an analysis of their correlation. She wants to ensure that her activities are in congruence with the goals. If she finds any discrepancies, she will have to find new activities to meet the goals within or outside of the virtual field trip, or she will have to adapt the goals to fit the available material.

Ms. Gifford decides that since this activity is but one supplemental activity for the overall Shakespeare unit, unless there is a significant discrepancy between the goals and the activities, she will not put in additional time toward searching for more Web sites to meet all of the original goals. This is a realistic position for any teacher to take when dealing with a supplemental activity. All teachers must find the fine line between the amount of work required for a project and the educational benefit the activity will provide for their students.

Ms. Gifford takes a holistic view of this particular curriculum and decides that she will not discard the goals not met within the virtual field trip but rather integrate them into alternative places within the unit.

With this understanding in mind, Ms. Gifford conducts an analysis of her virtual field trip, concentrating on the goals, activities, and time frame she designed for the experience.

SkyLight Professional Development

Goals

1. Do the collected Internet sites still cover the original goals of the experience?

   Goal #1: At the end of the activity, the students will be able to analyze, synthesize, and evaluate the various historical and cultural aspects and components of the Shakespearean era and his work to see how his work was influenced by these factors.

   Yes, all of the planned activities address and meet this goal.

   Goal #2: At the end of the activity, the students will have a better appreciation of the culture surrounding both Shakespeare and his work.

   The cultural section of the activity, which comprises the majority of the experience, addresses and meets this goal.

2. Are there new goals that I need to add, based on unexpected material that I discovered?

   Yes—based on the Internet site on Shakespeare's life that I discovered, I can add a third goal.

   Goal #3: At the end of the activity, the students will be able to know and understand the various important events of Shakespeare's life.

3. Are there goals that are no longer appropriate or feasible based on the sites that I did or did not find?

   No.

Activities

1. Are there sufficient URLs for the students to visit for each activity that is planned?

   No, I did not locate any material for the area titled "Political Climate: Policies."

2. If not, is there time or desire to continue the search for additional sites, or should I drop the proposed activity from the Internet session?

   This particular area is not overly important to the activity or to the stated goals. I can easily cover this material through other means—either by using the textbook or working with the students' history teachers. Therefore, I will not take additional search time to find additional sites for this activity.

3. Do some of the sites suggest additional activities that I should now add to the virtual field trip?

   Yes, a couple of sites suggest that I can add the following new categories:
   - *Culture: Architecture (Site to include: Castles on the Web)*
   - *The Plays: Shakespeare the Man (Site to include: Shakespeare the Man: Life and Times)*

Time Frame

1. Is the original anticipated time frame sufficient for using all of the Web sites that I selected?

   Probably not. There is a large amount of good material on each of these sites, and there are multiple sites for most activities. Each site could easily occupy an interested student for a significant amount of time, much longer than the two allotted days.

2. Do I need to adjust the time frame up or down?

   After checking with the computer lab teacher, it is impossible to add additional time to the activity—the lab is already reserved by another teacher. Students will only have the original two days (two periods of forty-eight minutes each) for the virtual field trip.

3. Do I need to add or delete sites to adjust to the time scheduled for the online experience?

To expedite the process within the time frame allowed, I need to reduce the number of sites for each activity so that there are only one or two sites designated per activity. I will link Internet sites that contain material for more than one area to only one of the activities instead of to all of them. If the students find a site that they really enjoy, they can still make the choice to investigate the other areas the site offers, whether the areas are linked to the original activity. As an additional alternative, I will provide a list of the Web sites and their URLs to students so they can research further on their own at home or in the school library media center.

The following is a list of the Internet sites that Ms. Gifford selects to represent each of the activities on the virtual field trip. All of the subcategories except "Daily Life" have only one site linked to the virtual field trip:

Culture
- Architecture: Castles on the Web
- Art: Medieval Art and Architecture
- Clothing: Exhibits Collection
- Daily Life: Wharram and Wichamstow (two sites)
- Dance: Exhibits Collection
- Food: Medieval & Renaissance Food Page
- Music: Medieval & Renaissance Instruments

The Plays
- Actors: Shakespeare's Globe
- Performances: Shakespeare's Globe
- Shakespeare the Man: Life and Times of William Shakespeare

Political Climate
- Rulers: Mr. William Shakespeare and the Internet

Making a Logical Plan to Implement the Shakespeare Virtual Field Trip

Now that Ms. Gifford has ensured that the virtual field trip is educationally sound, matching the goals and time frames, her next task is to plan the actual implementation of the trip. This includes the following:
- Determine how students will conduct the virtual field trip, including the time limitations within the trip
- Determine the activity's place within the overall curricular unit

Ms. Gifford has to ascertain how her students will experience the virtual field trip; in other words, how they will conduct the trip. She decides that rather than conducting the trip as a full class students will conduct the trip on an individualized basis in the computer lab activity to accommodate students' personal interests. This allows students to make their own decisions of which sites to visit and when to visit them, rather than having to direct them step by step. To start them off, Ms. Gifford decides to give a short introduction to the initial page of the field trip.

For the basis of the trip, Ms. Gifford decides to create a simple map of a typical medieval village. She asks the computer lab teacher to show her how to do this. The process is, in fact, much easier than she anticipated:

1. First, she scans a hand drawn picture that contains some sort of representation for each of the activities on the trip and saves it as a web-page graphic, called a gif (see Figure 4.9).
2. Using an easy-to-use Web-page creation program, she places hyperlinks within the appropriate spot in the picture, with each one leading to one of the URLs she selected.
3. For links embedded with a home page, she sets the hyperlink to go to that exact location, bypassing the home page.

Now that she knows how to create a hyperlink (a simple process that involves a couple of mouse clicks and typing in the URL to link to), the construction of the page for the virtual Web site goes surprisingly fast.

With this part completed, she asks the teacher who manages the school Web site to upload her page onto the school's Web site. Then she asks the computer lab aide to bookmark the page on all of the computers, so the computers are ready for students to use when they enter the lab.

SkyLight Professional Development

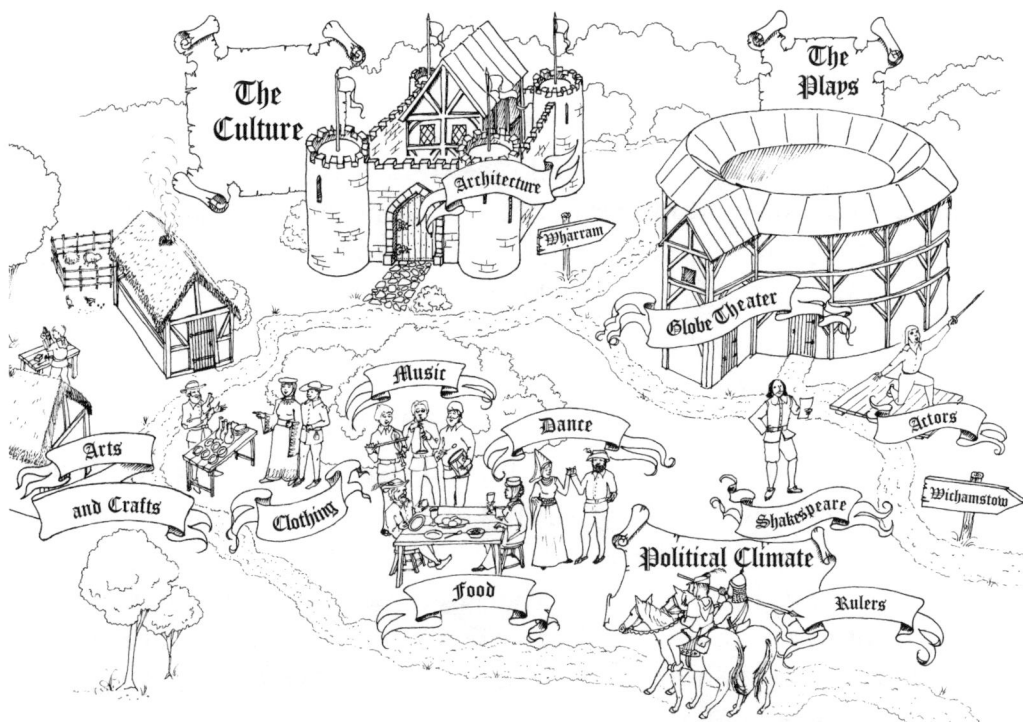

Figure 4.9

As far as time limitations, Ms. Gifford decides there will not be any, outside of the two days spent in the computer lab. She will not make any of the URLs mandatory for students to visit. Students can spend as much or as little time as they choose at each of the activities on the field trip. The only direction that she will give is that they should at least look at every site to determine if they have any interest in that particular activity. Since Ms. Gifford will tie in the virtual field trip to a culminating project (the booth project mentioned earlier), it behooves students to at least check out the various possibilities offered within the experience.

Even though students will have to do additional outside research for their projects, Ms. Gifford will tell them not to waste time copying down the URLs of sites that they want to use later. After the activity is complete, she will provide students with a complete list of the Web sites used in the virtual field trip.

Finally, after Ms. Gifford plans the entire trip, she needs to place it within the entire overall curricular unit concerning Shakespeare. This is the key to an overall valid and valuable curricular virtual field trip, and the question she needs to answer if administrators or parents have any doubts about why she will spend two full days on this activity. There are four basic ar-

Creating a Virtual Field Trip from Start to Finish

eas that she needs to determine and evaluate: activities before the trip, activities after the trip, activities not covered by the trip, and activities the trip now covers.

Learning Activities Before the Trip

1. What curricular areas do I need to cover before students embark on the virtual field trip?

   The students already have a basic knowledge of Shakespeare and his times, coming mostly from the introduction to their reading of Romeo and Juliet. They also have a limited knowledge of medieval times as a result of their history curriculum.

2. What prior knowledge do students need to ensure that they have the most productive educational experience possible?

   Again, they need some basic knowledge of medieval times, along with some limited background of the overall mores and life in Shakespeare's England. They received most of this background from their introduction to the play Romeo and Juliet and from viewing the movie, which gave somewhat accurate portrayals of Shakespeare's characters.

Learning Activities After the Trip

1. What extensions of the trip can I initiate after the students conclude?

   The students will select some aspect of life and culture of that time and creating a booth displaying the information. The booth will have a poster board display and possibly an artifact or two, or at least pictures, exemplifying their topics. The basis of this material will come from the areas that they study on the virtual field trip.

2. What curricular areas will students need to investigate based on the questions or problems that the trip experience may raise?

SkyLight Professional Development

The students will probably have to do additional research on the topic they select, seeing as the majority of their computer lab time will be spent investigating topics rather than research information. However, I will give them all of the URLs that the field trip uses, which they can then use to investigate more fully on their own, either at home (where approximately one-third of them have Internet access), in the school library/media center during nutrition or lunch or after school, or at the neighborhood library, which is Internet connected. In addition, they can use other sources for their research, such as an encyclopedia.

3. What assessment tools will I use to determine what students learned as a result of the virtual field trip?

I will use the students' original booths, based on the cultural experiences that they acquired from the virtual field trip as the primary assessment tool for the activity. I will create a rubric to formally grade the projects, taking into account quality and quantity of sources used, along with the students' analysis, synthesis, and evaluation of the various aspects and components of the Shakespearean era. I will make an informal, qualitative assessment of any change in their appreciation of Shakespearean material based on their attitudes toward the reading of the play and subsequent Shakespearean lessons and activities.

Learning Activities Not Covered by the Trip

1. What curricular areas did I *not* cover in the trip that I need to introduce, using some other teaching methodology: direct instruction, cooperative learning, or the use of classroom materials such as the textbook or other supplemental items?

There are two basic curricular areas that the virtual field trip does not cover. One is a study of actual Shakespearean text, which students are doing within the classroom as a literature study. The second area involves a more detailed study of the political culture of that time, which students are doing in a more efficient and effective way within the history curriculum.

SkyLight Professional Development

Creating a Virtual Field Trip from Start to Finish

Learning Activities Now Covered by the Trip

1. What unanticipated curricular areas does the trip provide that I no longer need to cover or duplicate in other areas of the unit?

   Areas that I no longer need to cover in the rest of the unit include Shakespearean culture. Through the use of the virtual field trip and subsequent assignment, the students will gain most of the curricular material necessary for this unit for Shakespearean English culture. In addition, I can spend less time on a study of Shakespeare himself since this is now included within the activity.

Checking for Multiple Intelligences

Finally, Ms. Gifford verifies that the virtual field trip targets multiple intelligences within the unit. She is well aware of the value in ensuring that all of her activities target different ways of learning. Ms. Gifford determines that she incorporates each intelligence into the overall unit on *Romeo and Juliet* (see Figure 4.10).

Unexpectedly, Ms. Gifford discovers that the virtual field trip integrates many of the intelligences into her students' experiences and does so much easier than in her normal, everyday classroom curricular situations. This is especially the case with a number of the areas in which she often has trouble incorporating, such as bodily/kinesthetic, musical/rhythmic, and intrapersonal intelligences.

Assessing the Product

Ms. Gifford constructs a rubric to use with the assessment of the booths assignment. Since this particular project is so creative and requires the students to incorporate the higher order thinking skills of application, analysis, synthesis, and evaluation, she makes the rubric simple, knowing that she will base much of the assessment on subjective decisions, relying on her expertise as an educator in this area. The areas that she decides to cover in the rubric are as follows:
- Overall creative effort in construction of the booth
- Use of a variety of medium

SkyLight Professional Development

VIRTUAL FIELD TRIPS IN THE CYBERAGE

- Presentation of cultural aspect chosen
- Use of material from more than one Internet site

She decides to score each area on a four point system (see Figure 4.11). She will obtain some of this data from personal observation and oral discussions with the individual students as she peruses their booths.

As far as the actual value of the virtual field trip experience itself, Ms. Gifford knows that her teaching experience and knowledge of this class

Multiple Intelligences Checklist
Unit: Shakespeare—His Life and Times

INTELLIGENCE	CURRICULAR LOCATION
Verbal/Linguistic	Reading the play *Romeo and Juliet*
Logical/Mathematical	The virtual field trip and subsequent booth activity—exploring various items, manipulating data and materials
Visual/Spatial	The virtual field trip—viewing pictures and images
Bodily/Kinesthetic	Learning about medieval dance on the trip; learning a folk dance I discovered during my investigation, which I can teach during the booth day
Musical/Rhythmic	Learning about medieval instruments on the trip; learning a song found during my investigation
Interpersonal	Cooperative group work within the unit
Intrapersonal	The virtual field trip—individual choices made during personal exploration time on the activity
Naturalist	Classifying and categorizing data from the virtual field trip

Figure 4.10

Creating a Virtual Field Trip from Start to Finish

Rubric				
Criteria	no effort	minimal effort	required effort	exceptional effort
Overall creative effort in construction of the booth	unorganized presentation	minimal organization	presentation organized	presentation well-organized and well-executed
Use of a variety of medium	1 type	2 types	3 types	4 types
Presentation of cultural aspect chosen	aspect unclear	somewhat clear	aspect clear	aspect shows exceptional level of clarity
Use of material from more than one Internet site	1 site	2 sites	3 sites	4 sites

Figure 4.11

(her educational connoisseurship) will immediately and instinctively tell her how well students implement their projects.

Now satisfied that she has planned the virtual field trip as impeccably as possible, she is ready to share the experience with her students.

Why Did She Spend All of This Time?

Why did Ms. Gifford spend all of this time planning a short two-day, supplemental virtual field trip assignment? Besides the obvious reason—an enhanced curricular experience for her students in an area that they would not have acquired otherwise—the answer is quite simple.

First of all, the preparation really did not take as much time as it may seem. The entire process of planning, investigating, and constructing a virtual field trip usually takes between five and ten hours, depending on the availability of the resources, teachers' personal levels of expertise with the Internet, and the depth and creativity into which teachers want to delve.

SkyLight Professional Development

Teachers can handwrite all of their checklists and tables and draw the web on a blank sheet of paper, making revisions by crossing out or using correction fluid.

Ms. Gifford made the majority of the decisions (written out above for the reader) in her head, using the extensive teaching repertoire that she has developed through her teacher preparatory classes and classroom experience. Many of the decision points came to her innately with little conscience thought.

Still, it may seem like an unusual amount of effort for a short supplementary activity, but not when it is put into context. Ms. Gifford did two important things with her virtual field trip:

1. Ms. Gifford can save the information—URLs, webs, tables—for the following year, when she is to teach Shakespeare again. She realizes that a number of the sites may change over the course of the year, still, most will probably stay the same. She can easily replace those sites that change through the use of the search engines and general education sites. She has already completed the vast majority of the legwork, adapting the trip for the following year will be relatively simple.

2. She can share the virtual field trip with other Internet-using language arts teachers, letting them use it with their classes. Many teachers may be so enamored with the concept, that they will construct their own based on the units they are doing later in the year. Of course, they can then share their work with Ms. Gifford and her students. Soon other teachers in other content areas may construct virtual field trips and share the material with their colleagues, significantly reducing the amount of overall work that any one teacher has to do. Teachers may even get together to create virtual field trips that cross the curriculum.

The result of Ms. Gifford's effort was a number of teenagers, previously bored to death with the entire concept of Shakespeare, were fully involved in learning about his life and times and were now turned on to the study of the culture of that period. The ultimate evaluation of the worth of this activity came from a student who had previously disliked *Romeo and Juliet*, when he excitedly asked Ms. Gifford, "When can we read another Shakespeare play?"

SkyLight Professional Development

HOW TO INTEGRATE VIRTUAL FIELD TRIPS INTO THE CURRICULUM

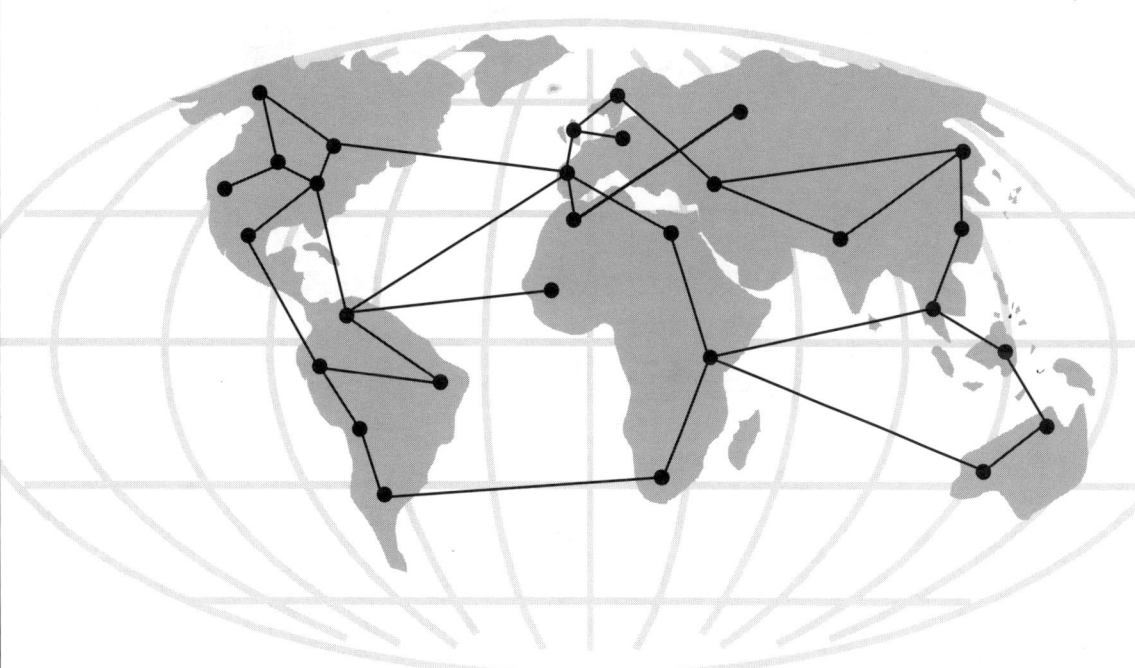

CHAPTER FIVE

CHAPTER 5

How to Integrate Virtual Field Trips into the Curriculum

....

The Shape of Society

Mr. Yasinow* wants his students to comprehend the connection between mathematics and the real world. As modern middle school students, they see little practical application for mathematics outside of knowing how to use a calculator and how to balance a checkbook. For students whose parents have a checkbook type program on their home computers, even the latter function is obsolete.

Mr. Yasinow decides that he will take his students on a virtual field trip into the world of geometry. He wants to show them how geometric theories have practical applications within society. He can accomplish this by showing students various forms of architecture that exemplify the use of geometry.

Mr. Yasinow first searches for a number of Internet sites that contain various examples and pictures of buildings. He is looking for those that explicitly incorporate geometric shapes in their design. Since he is well aware that there are a large number of architecturally oriented sites on the Internet, he decides to start his search with YAHOO!, which normally contains the best of all of the official architectural locations.

* All names of teachers are fictional.

In the YAHOO! index, he first looks at the "Arts & Humanities" category, then follows the links first to "Design Arts," then to "Architecture," and finally to "Buildings and Structures." On that page he discovers over fifty sites concerning the area of architecture. Among them are the following useful sites, each of which contains pictures of structures that incorporate a variety of geometric shapes:

Chicago Cultural Center - architectural showplace for the lively and visual arts, presenting more than 1,000 free programs and exhibitions annually.

Eiffel Tower@ (Please note that YAHOO! uses the notation "@" after a link, rather than a description, when that link is actually a file of various sites, rather than one specific URL.)

Great Pyramid - essay on the oldest structure on earth.

Independence Hall@

Joy of Concrete, The - links to buildings made from concrete.

Poplar Forest - Thomas Jefferson's personal retreat. Explore the octagonal house and learn about the restoration under way and the discoveries of archaeologists.

Rundetaarn, The Round Tower - in Copenhagen, Denmark. King Chr. IV's famous tower. Music, exhibitions, observatory and more.

Rural Impressions - follow a student across the US on a bike while examining the architectural developments of rural America.

Taj Mahal@

Tower of Pisa@

United States Capitol@

World Federation of Great Towers - association of international monuments working together to foster awareness and develop local and international opportunities for promotion.

SkyLight Professional Development

Now that he has this extensive list of sites, he puts together a scavenger hunt of the geometrically designed buildings. The students then pair up into teams. Mr. Yasinow gives each team a list of two and three dimensional figures to locate, the list of URLs, and an hour of search time. The team that locates and prints out the greatest number of examples wins.

Not only is the experience a huge success, but students use the material that they find as real-life examples within their classwork, particularly in lessons involving area, polygons, surface area, volume, angles, and symmetry. Mr. Yasinow's students discover dozens of examples of geometry in architecture. Ultimately, although reluctantly, they finally admit that mathematics actually *is* relevant in today's society.

Where to Begin?

This chapter is designed to give teachers some starting points for generating ideas for their own personal virtual field trips. Chapters 1 and 2 explain why virtual field trips are important; chapters 3 and 4 explain how to make personal virtual field trips. This chapter and the next help answer the question of how to integrate virtual field trips into curricular subject matter.

The basic goal of this chapter is to spark ideas within teachers' minds. Teachers should not use this chapter or the following one as a virtual directory of field trips—where teachers can pick out trips and use them as is. Rather, the material in these pages provides initial ideas to spark teachers' creativity and to steer them toward integrating virtual field trips into their classroom curricula. As teachers scan through these pages, they can think of how to adapt the ideas presented to their own curricula to make the experiences truly personal.

The ideas on these pages are presented in as general a form as possible, while intermingled with some specific examples of how teachers can go about the actual process. The listings are by far not all inclusive. There are many potential areas within each subject area that the material does not touch on. This chapter focuses on five major curricular ar-

eas: language arts, social studies/history, science, mathematics, and the arts.

Language Arts

Virtual field trips, as exemplified in the previous chapter, can greatly expand students' knowledge and experience within the language arts. This section focuses on three basic parts of the language arts curriculum in which virtual field trips have the greatest benefit: literature, authors and poets, and student creative writing.

Literature

Literature is one of the most prolific areas in which to integrate virtual field trips. Within a virtual field trip, teachers can take students into the setting of the novel: either back in time or to a far different location. An online experience can serve as the major resource of supplemental material for a literary work, as was shown in the earlier Shakespeare example (see chapter 4).

Some topics are easily accessible within a virtual field trip, such as taking a trip to the South Pacific as a prelude to reading *Island of the Blue Dolphin* (O'Dell 1990). However, some topics are much more problematic and difficult to create, such as trying to develop a trip to the rural south during the time of *To Kill A Mockingbird* (Lee 1960). Teachers can consider the balance between the benefits of a virtual field trip and the effort needed to locate materials on their topics. The following are a few fundamental considerations to use in making this basic decision:

- Present day locations around the world are very easy to use as a virtual field trip topic
- Events or locations back in time are more difficult to use as a virtual field trip topic

Present Day Locations

There are currently picture-laden Internet sites for practically every spot in the world that has electricity. Even a country as small and remote as Nepal, located in the heart of the Himalayas, has 175 different Internet sites

How to Integrate Virtual Field Trips into the Curriculum

registered with YAHOO! Since YAHOO! carries the vast majority of official governmental and large commercial sites dealing with locations around the world, it is the easiest place to start constructing a field trip of this type.

In the YAHOO! index there is a heading titled "Regional." Under that heading, select the most appropriate place: country, region, or U.S. state. This index contains most of the materials and links that teachers will want for their virtual field trips.

Past Events or Locations

Basically, the more well-known or broad an event or time period is the easier it is to locate material. The key to finding this type of information is to use the social studies collections of sites for the material.

If students are reading *Sarah, Plain and Tall* (Maclachlan 1985) and the teacher wants to locate materials on pioneer life in the 1890s, the easiest place to find this information is the HISTORY/SOCIAL STUDIES WEB SITE FOR K-12 TEACHERS. First going to "American History Sources," then to the "Native Americans and the Frontier West" link, provides dozens of usable sites covering every aspect of pioneer culture imaginable—from the concept of mail-order brides (the main subject of the novel) to examples of the soddies that the pioneers lived in on the plains. The following are two more examples of relevant sites:

Crossing the Frontier
Includes more than 300 images of the American West dating from 1849 to the present that document ". . . changes in the ways we have represented and idealized the vast Western landscape over the last 140 years, from a place of boundless beauty and limitless opportunity . . . to a landscape hemmed in by suburbanization and sometimes tinged with a tragic sense of loss." Under educational resources, the site provides special information on how to use the site information in the classroom. Possible integration topics include: Westward migration and the colliding of cultures in the American West, the growth of Western cities, the history of science and technology in the U. S., the Gold Rush.

Gallery of the Open Frontier
An image library of photos, paintings, and drawings on American Western history. See the Special Listings Menu—Children on the Frontier, Dams and Canals, Trains and Railroads, Sod Houses and Other Homesteads, Native Americans, Studio Photographs, Schools, Farming, Construction Projects.

SkyLight Professional Development

While a virtual field trip of this nature is excellent for exemplifying broad cultural and historical events, it is much more difficult for dealing with more narrow issues, such as was mentioned about studying the rural south during the time of *To Kill a Mockingbird*. There is little material either in print or online concerning the narrow topics of racism in the south in the early 1900s or on the southern rural poor before World War II. Generally speaking, if printed curricular material on a subject exists, chances are that teachers can also now find it on the Internet.

Nonetheless, virtual field trips are an invaluable assistance for providing supplemental material for the background and settings of a great many works of literature.

Authors and Poets

Virtual field trips can provide material about the experiences of authors and poets. It is especially beneficial for students to comprehend the writers' environments in which they have lived or currently live that influence their work. This is a particularly important exercise when dealing with an author who is recognizable by the settings of his prose or poetry such as Mark Twain, who wrote about life long ago on the Mississippi River, or Robert Frost, who wrote extensively on life in New England.

If students are doing a lesson on a novel by Mark Twain, understanding the location and lifestyle of the inhabitants of Hannibal, Missouri, greatly adds to students' understanding of the novel. An easy way to accomplish this is with a field trip to Hannibal. Since Hannibal is considered a municipality, YAHOO! is the most logical place to begin.

In the YAHOO! index, teachers can first select the category, "Regional," then "US States," "Missouri," "Cities," and finally "Hannibal." To learn about life in this area, teachers can select "Community." Under this subheading, teachers can click on "Guides." The following Internet site appears and contains all of the information necessary for a virtual field trip, along with an assortment of additional helpful links:

> **Hannibal, Missouri**—provides historical and current city information as well as in depth visitor details and guides.

The same basic process works with a study of the environment and community of Robert Frost. Since Frost dealt with an entire region, New

SkyLight Professional Development

England, the search is not quite as straightforward as investigating an individual city. Teachers can, of course, select a typical New England city and use that location as an example. However, teachers may want to investigate the entire region, if at all feasible.

YAHOO! can also assist with this search. By using the category "Regional" once again, teachers can select the subcategory "Regions," then "U.S. Regions," and finally "New England." This page includes categories in all different areas, along with the following specialized Web sites that prove useful for creating a virtual field trip about Robert Frost's environmental inspiration:

Abbington Village—Shop for products "made in New England" and gather information on what to see and do, and where to stay and play in New England.

Explore New England

New England Information Network—Travel, living, and visiting information.

Virtual New England—travel, shops, real estate, and events.

Yankee Web Explorer, The

Of course, teachers can also search on METACRAWLER for "Robert Frost," securing numerous Web sites about the man and his work. Many of these sites may also contain relevant information about the poet. However, if teachers' primary goals are to discover information about the region in which he wrote, then a YAHOO! search for New England is the best place to start.

Background information on authors and poets is one way to incorporate virtual Web sites into literature. Unfortunately, this is not quite as helpful when the author is eclectic in setting—when there is no one place or region that really defines the writer. Luckily, many writers now have their own Internet sites that provide a good deal of personal information about that author, including an examination of their writing and thought processes. In this respect, teachers can have the students go on a virtual field trip to a writer's "home" in conjunction with a literature unit. This process works especially well with authors of children's books.

SkyLight Professional Development

The easiest way to locate information of this nature is to use the CHILDREN'S LITERATURE WEB GUIDE, which teachers can find on the Educational Resources page of the general educational site TEACHERS HELPING TEACHERS. This exercise leads to some remarkable information especially when researching authors who primarily write for children, such as Judy Blume.

By clicking on the "Authors on the Web" link to the CHILDREN'S LITERATURE WEB GUIDE, teachers discover a specialized link to Judy Blume:

JUDY BLUME'S OFFICIAL WEB SITE—designed for kids

This specialized site contains the following wonderful links for use in a virtual field trip to the author's house:
- A Message from Judy
- Favorite Questions for Judy
- Guest Book
- What's New
- Bio and Photos
- Judy's Books
- Related Links
- Dive in to the Special KIDS Page!!

Judy Blume, as well as other authors and poets, can unexpectedly come alive for younger students.

Student Writing

Older students can turn creative writing and research papers into virtual field trips. They can demonstrate examples of their material by linking appropriate Internet sites into their work. This phenomenon works especially well in some of the newer word processing programs that automatically create hyperlinks to Web sites simply by typing in a URL.

To incorporate such virtual online material into their writing, students can search for sites during a researching session. To start, teachers can show students how to use METACRAWLER, which greatly speeds up the research process since it provides a list of the top sites from all of the major search engines.

SkyLight Professional Development

If students are writing science fiction stories, they might want to attach one of the links discovered at the NASA Web site into their work. Students can easily enhance an original story of life on Mars with a connection to the "Multi-media gallery" at the NASA Internet site.

Even elementary students can supplement their writing with an Internet experience. If students are studying *The Jungle Book* (Kipling 1894), teachers can help students create an additional story involving Mowgli and the other characters as a supplemental activity. Students can easily integrate a visit to a tiger's habitat into their work by typing in the search term "tiger" into METACRAWLER. The search provides the following excellent site that students can add to their material:

Tiger Information Center
Excite: The Tiger Information Center is dedicated to providing information to help preserve the remaining five subspecies of tigers. To learn more about tigers, just click on the topic below. If you have more questions, email us. http://www.5tigers.org/ (Excite, Infoseek, WebCrawler)

Older students can implement the same process within a topical research paper. If students are writing formal research papers, they can include links to virtual field trips on various topics, such as a location or a place in time. This is similar to students adding an appendix of additional information to their report.

In any event, there are numerous possibilities for incorporating virtual field trips into language arts, especially in curricular areas involving literature, authors and poets, and student writing.

Social Studies/History

Probably the easiest subject area to implement a virtual field trip is the vast area contained within the social studies/history curricula. The three major topic areas of this part of the curriculum are the studies of the community (elementary grades), United States and world history (upper elementary grades through high school), and the humanities (primarily high school). United States and world history are combined in the following examples since the process of implementing virtual field trips is quite similar between the two (Mandel 1998).

The Community

A virtual field trip to various communities is an extremely easy process to create. The previous example of using YAHOO! to search Hannibal, Missouri, illustrates this process (see language arts). However, often the curriculum involves a study of the school's own particular community or city. A virtual field trip is an excellent way of giving students a personal experience when the school's budget cannot.

In Los Angeles, The Getty Center, a multibillion dollar art museum, recently opened. Although the museum is a fantastic place for all students to visit, most schools cannot afford more than one or two field trips during the school year. Elementary schools may not even consider The Getty Center as a top choice. Luckily, students can experience this museum through a virtual field trip.

Using METACRAWLER and the search term "Getty Center," students immediately find the following link:

Getty, The
Infoseek: The Getty offers opportunities to more fully understand,
Yahoo!: through a museum, five institutes and a grant program, the Getty provides opportunities for people to more fully understand, experience, value, and preserve the world's art and cultural heritage.
http://www.getty.edu/ (Infoseek, Yahoo!)

Using this link, along with a subsequent one marked "Online Tour," students are suddenly at the museum looking at many of the exhibits and designs they would see if they were actually there. If teachers have access to projection screen monitors, the experience is even more realistic. Students can actually experience the museum without setting foot in the building.

Using the Internet, teachers can enhance the virtual field trip experience in ways that a real trip to the museum cannot provide. For example, the Getty Center has a beautiful circular garden designed by Robert Irwin, one that is sure to catch students' attention. If teachers want to extend the field trip experience, they can go to the WORLD WIDE ARTS RESOURCES, search for "Irwin," and find additional examples of this artist's work that students can study.

Teachers can implement online community field trips with countless examples in every major city and most small towns, too. In addition, a virtual field trip can help link supplemental material to the curricular experience.

In lower grades, students can study many community-type professions, such as firefighters, police officers, or doctors. Teachers can easily take students on a virtual field trip to visit these people all over the country. Since YAHOO! contains most municipal Internet sites, it is the logical place to start. If teachers search "firefighters" on YAHOO!, they find the overall category of

Health: Public Health and Safety: Fire Protection

If teachers click that link, they find an additional link to the category "Fire Companies," which by itself contains Internet sites for 323 different fire companies around the country. Teachers can easily select one of these fire company sites for their students to visit. On many of these sites, teachers can even personalize the trip by having students correspond with a firefighter through e-mail. Ultimately, this experiential process works with any number of professions that early elementary students study as part of their curricula.

United States and World History

The process of incorporating virtual field trips into United States and world history is similar to that described earlier in the Boston Tea Party example (see chapter 3). A combination of searches using YAHOO!, METACRAWLER, and general-education and subject-matter Web sites leads teachers to the vast majority of the information and material that is needed to construct such an experience. The HISTORY/SOCIAL SOCIAL WEB SITE FOR K-12 TEACHERS and the HISTORICAL TEXT ARCHIVE also prove to be two of the most indispensable Internet sites available to teachers constructing virtual field trips.

Complex, multileveled virtual field trips, such as the Boston Tea Party example, are not the only option for teachers. Based on the amount of work needed to construct one of them, it is hard to imagine that teachers would use such an involved trip more than on a periodic basis throughout the year. Teachers can integrate the same principles of such an activity on a one-day basis. Teachers can easily create smaller, one- or two-stop virtual field trips to enhance the everyday history curriculum, with minimum effort. There are online possibilities for use in virtually any topic. Here are a number of curricular examples, using the HISTORY/SOCIAL SOCIAL WEB SITE

VIRTUAL FIELD TRIPS IN THE CYBERAGE

FOR K-12 TEACHERS as the source to locate Web sites for the study of various historical topics and time periods:

- Ancient Egypt: Take the students on a tour of Ancient Egypt at THE ANCIENT EGYPTIAN CULTURE EXHIBIT. They can enjoy an experience as they take a virtual field trip of ancient Egyptian daily life, the military, the arts or architecture of the time.
- The Byzantine Empire: Take the students on a virtual tour of the art and icons of that time and how this work exemplified the religious aspect of the Byzantine Period at the Internet site BYZANTINE RELIGIOUS ICONOGRAPHY AND ICON ART.
- Civil Rights: Take the students to a speech given by Malcolm X at the University of Berkeley in 1963. They can hear an actual recording of his words at the site AUDIO ONLINE: STREAMED AUDIO FILES, MEDIA RESOURCES CENTER, UCB.
- Holocaust: Take the students on a virtual tour of the ghetto experience, the concentration camps and other aspects of the Holocaust at A TEACHER'S GUIDE TO THE HOLOCAUST. Also included is a section on the arts, where students can download music from the Holocaust period or take a tour of a gallery of children's art work that was created in the camps.
- The Napoleonic Era: Take the students on a tour of this French leader's life, battles and an investigation of many additional aspects of his overall history at THE NAPOLEON SERIES: LIFE & TIMES OF NAPOLEON BONEPARTE.
- The Spanish-American War: Take the students on a tour of the battleship Maine, whose sinking was the instigator of the Spanish-American War. Go to the REMEMBER THE MAINE Internet site to see a narrated pictorial history of the ship, event and the yellow journalism that followed, all of which led the United States into the war.

Teachers do not need a lengthy virtual field trip project to give the students an online experience. Short, one-day trips require a minimum amount of teacher preparation are readily available in nearly all areas of historical study.

How to Integrate Virtual Field Trips into the Curriculum

The Humanities

Many teachers describe the humanities as the various topics within social studies that do not fit into the previously discussed areas. This includes topics such as government, cultural studies, and comparative religions to name a few. Most of the nonhistory-based social studies courses in high school curricula are often placed under the umbrella category of the humanities.

The humanities are an excellent place to integrate virtual field trips. There are numerous places on the Internet where students can expand their knowledge and experiences within the various topic areas. A sampling of examples that deal with the areas of democracy, multicultural studies, and current events follow.

Democracy

Since the curricular area of the humanities is so broad, there is not a model to work from. Students gain a good deal of Internet experience simply from their individual teacher's curriculum, along with the personal creativity of the student. Luckily, there are many places where teachers can turn to find material for these subject areas.

The concept of democracy is an excellent example and one often explicitly found within the secondary curriculum. Students can experience first-hand the democratic process through the use of an Internet site such as **THE JEFFERSON PROJECT**. This site contains the following goals, information, and links:

> The Jefferson Project is a public service that Net.Capitol, Inc. provides to help stimulate the electronic public discourse. Believing that a democracy requires the broadest possible participation, Net.Capitol maintains this collection of political sites and public fora. In here, you should find everything you need to become an involved member of the American democracy.
> - Do-it-yourself Politics—Roll up your sleeves and get active!
> - State Resources—State-by-state listing of local Internet government and political resources.
> - Political Parties—Local and national party sites.
> - Political Humor—Admit it, it's funny.
> - The Left—If you lean this way, go this way.

SkyLight Professional Development

- The Right—If you lean this way, go this way.
- The Issues—What are we arguing about?
- Government Resources—How does the government use the Internet, and how can you use those resources?
- Political Watchdogs—Who watches the watchmen?
- International Resources—We're not alone.
- Voicebox—Make your voice heard! A public forum for debating our national issues.
- CapWeb Classic—Find your representatives using the search engine that powers Net.Capitol's CapWeb Custom.

An easy virtual field trip that teachers can construct is to have students attend a town hall meeting with representatives from the various political parties in attendance. Teachers can simply link dissimilar positions of different parties, as espoused within the Web site links above. The students can go from one person to another as they learn about the various topics. During presidential election years, students can attend the Democratic or Republican convention by going to those respective parties' Web sites and studying the issues and the candidates, even following the actual itinerary of the convention.

Through various experiences such as those described above, students can get a firsthand working knowledge of how democracy manifests itself within American society.

Multicultural Studies

Multicultural studies are a major focus of the humanities today. Numerous secondary and elementary schools offer or integrate studies of comparative cultures, religions, and regions into the curriculum. Teachers can construct virtual field trips in any of these areas on any level to provide students with a better understanding of the phenomenon.

A popular and basic example is the study of Cinco de Mayo, the Latin American celebration that almost every grade level throughout many regions of the United States observes. Students can easily experience an online celebration of this day while using the Internet.

If teachers type in the term "Cinco de Mayo" into METACRAWLER, they would find the following links and descriptions:

Cinco De Mayo
Excite, WebCrawler: On May 5th my family celebrates Cinco de Mayo. First we go to church, then we have a special dinner with all kinds of different food. We eat enchiladas, tacos, sopa, and my aunt makes a special punch that is delicious. http://intergate.bcsd.k12.ca.us/fremont/h5mayo.htm (Excite, WebCrawler)

NOBLE Web: Cinco de Mayo
NOBLE Web Cinco De Mayo Cinco de Mayo- The story of Cinco de Mayo from Latinonet Cinco de Mayo History— UCLA's Cinco de Mayo http://www.noble.mass.edu/tty5cin.htm (Lycos)

Infoseek: Cinco de Mayo
Get homework help, parenting tips, events and activities for the kids, holiday fun, and more. http://guide.infoseek.com/Kids . . . ys_and_festivals/Cinco_de_Mayo (Excite)

Cinco de Mayo Fiesta Official Site
V111 Annual Cinco de Mayo Fiesta in Downtown Pasco, WA 1997 FlowerThe Official SiteFlower VIII Cinco de Mayo Fiesta in D. http://www.sired.com/cinco97/ (Lycos)

These are only a few of the offerings. There are many more sites covering a variety of multicultural holidays. Teachers can easily construct a full, multicultural virtual field trip incorporating multiple intelligences using these Internet locations. For example, teachers can create maps of community parks filled with booths and other locations that are linked to sites containing Cinco de Mayo material such as art, music, stories, history of the holiday, and other cultural information.

Teachers can develop similar experiences using material from other religions, cultures, and people around the world to provide students with experiences that they could normally not acquire without physically being at the particular location.

Current Events

Current events is one of the easiest areas from which to construct a virtual field trip experience, and it is a topic found in almost every grade starting with elementary school. Luckily, there are a number of news sites that are extremely useful, especially CNN INTERACTIVE, a site that seems to be designed for student use.

SkyLight Professional Development

CNN INTERACTIVE contains links for almost every possible area of current events, including most related and side topics to the particular story. Teachers can use these links to create a virtual "news magazine" on a particular current topic or a news broadcast on a variety of selected issues; the possibilities are endless.

Regardless of the topic, teachers can design virtual field trips in every area imaginable within the humanities. Teachers can easily construct curricular lessons to greatly enhance an already very experiential curricular area, directly leading to greater student understanding and appreciation of the various topics.

Science

There is probably no greater number of virtual field trip resources than in the curricular area of the sciences. Previously constructed virtual field trips abound in this subject area, from excursions into rain forest habitats to journeys into the heart of volcanoes to visits to geological excavations.

There is even a special Internet site titled THE VIRTUAL FIELD TRIPS SITE. This site includes probably the best collection of ready-made educationally oriented virtual field trips on the Web. The site currently contains, or has plans to contain, fully constructed virtual field trips in the following curricular areas:

Beaches	Ponds
Bogs	Prairies
Construction Sites	Rain Forests
Deserts	Salt Marshes
Dinosaurs	Sharks
Farms	Streams
Glaciers	Tide pools
Hurricanes	Urban
Meadows	Volcanoes
Mountains	Whales
Natural Wonders of the World	Woods
Oceans	

Of the twenty-three field trip subject areas listed, at least twenty of them are predominantly science-related, as is the case with the vast majority of virtual field trip sites. Besides this particular Web site, there are numer-

ous other science-related sites on the Internet. Teachers can use these online activities either in their entirety, or they can supplement them with additional material for a more personalized experience for the students.

Unfortunately, the vast majority of these ready-made scientific-based sites involve only a narrow band of topics that primarily fall into four basic categories:

1. Biology Sites: Sites involving individual animal and plant species (such as the tiger example mentioned earlier), collections of animals (such as those found at zoological locations), and ecosystem experiences (such as the rain forest or oceans examples).
2. Space Exploration Sites: Sites involving planetary and galaxy exploration. The best of these sites are connected to NASA.
3. Geology Sites: Sites involving current geological trips around the world, where students can join the geologists. Also included are sites revolving around geological formations, such as volcanoes.
4. Geography Sites: Sites involving various weather phenomenon, such as tornadoes, hurricanes, along with those dealing with specialized climates, such as deserts and the Arctic and Antarctic regions.

Besides these sites, virtual museum experiences are another excellent source of virtual field trips. Again, the majority of these exist within the areas of the sciences. Most major museums such as the SMITHSONIAN INSTITUTE now offer virtual trips through their exhibits. In addition, there are a number of Internet sites that are purely online virtual museums.

One such Internet location is the FRANKLIN INSTITUTE SCIENCE MUSEUM that advertises itself as containing a world of virtual exhibits. The museum has numerous excellent experiential activities for students of all ages and is designed as if the students were walking through the museum itself. Other online activities include the following links and descriptions:

Flights of Inspiration celebrates the 95th anniversary of sustained, powered flight.

Visit the ocean with **Undersea and Oversee.**

Volcanoes erupt, the crust quakes, and rivers rage. **Earthforce** is everywhere.

Be your own neighborhood weather forecaster with **Franklin's Forecast,** an online exhibit about weather forecasting.

SkyLight Professional Development

Follow the action in one high school biology lab and you'll get the **BioPoint**. Mrs. Mazen's biology class is online, offering both the teacher and student points of view.

All of the above pages include information and activities along with additional links for a complete virtual museum experience on the Internet.

Another example of this type of virtual science experience is a site such as the EXPLORATORIUM. This site provides a new type of virtual field trip every three months dealing with a specific topic. The topic, at the time of printing, is chocolate and includes the following links:

Chocolate in the Forest—A visit to the Amazon, a source for chocolate.
An "American Invention"—The Olmecs, the Mayans, and Aztecs.
Chocolate Invades Europe—Chocolate conquers the continent.
From Bean to Bar—Take a video tour of the Scharffen Berger chocolate factory.
Health Help or Risk—Can chocolate help prevent heart disease?
"Feel Good" Food—More than a food but less than a drug.

Although not entirely science oriented, the site relates the topic in as many ways as possible to science and health. The topics change every three months; so check the site for updates. Links to previous topics include the following:
- Exploring Hair: "Better Hair Through Chemistry"
- Exploring Memories: "Young in Mind"

Unfortunately, there are few ready-made sites available for the curricular areas of chemistry or physics, other than as they relate to the sites above. Still, teachers can create virtual field trips in these areas as they would for any other subject area, using search engines, general educational sites, and subject-matter sites to accumulate appropriate online material. Seeing as there is such an abundance of science-oriented virtual field trips already established on the Internet, it behooves teachers to search the subject at hand as a first step, rather than recreating work already accomplished by others.

SkyLight Professional Development

How to Integrate Virtual Field Trips into the Curriculum

Mathematics

There are not many ready-to-use virtual field trips covering the area of mathematics. After all, it is easier to visit a volcano than it is to visit a quadratic equation. Still, there are a number of ways to integrate an Internet virtual experience into the mathematics curriculum (see A Tool or a Fad?). Although peripheral to the mathematics curriculum, two of the easiest possibilities are interviewing mathematicians and creating virtual critical thinking problems. A third option is to have students look at various experiential mathematical sites.

Mathematician Interviews

To have students interview a famous mathematician, teachers can create a virtual field trip as described earlier in the language arts examples concerning authors. Teachers link as much personal information and as many examples of the mathematician's work before students "sit down" with the person. Teachers can also construct this online experience as a panel of mathematicians presenting their work and theories. Teachers can use the searching tips previously outlined in this book (see chapter 2) to locate and integrate appropriate Internet sites.

Virtual Critical-Thinking Problems

Teachers can create virtual critical-thinking problems using almost any subject and grade level. Teachers can make them as simple as linking two pictures of cities, two pictures of trains, and a script describing their speed

---

A Tool or a Fad?

Too often in education, we take new innovations and integrate them into every possible facet of the curricula with the reasoning that educational gains of that innovation will automatically be present whenever that innovation is used.

Some curricular areas are more adaptable to them than others. It is quite easy to integrate virtual field trips into the history curriculum on all levels; it is quite a strain to integrate them into the mathematics curriculum on a regular basis.

You need to determine the usefulness of Internet activities toward meeting the goals of the curriculum, rather than simply creating a virtual experience because it is the thing to do.

This is not to say that you cannot integrate virtual field trips into the mathematics curriculum. Although current research stresses that the primary use of the Internet in mathematics is the incorporation of statistic analysis (Drier et al. 1999), a creative math teacher can design excellent ways to bring a virtual field trip experience into the classroom.

In other words, in all subject areas teachers need to first ask the question: *Why* am I planning this specific trip?

SkyLight Professional Development

and distance, along with the obvious question of how soon the two trains would meet.

Teachers can construct mathematical story problems around almost any online scenario, using preexisting or newly created sites. The primary benefit of this endeavor is the built-in motivational factor for getting the students involved with figuring out mathematical problems. Teachers can extend this experience with older students by giving them an Internet site or interesting scenarios and having them develop their own critical thinking problems. There is also a plethora of game and logic mathematics sites, such as INTERACTIVE MATHEMATICS ONLINE or THE MATH FORUM HOME PAGE, in which students can apply, analyze, and evaluate the mathematics concepts associated with the game or puzzle. Teachers can locate these types of sites through most of the general educational Internet sites.

Experiential Mathematical Sites

A final way of creating a virtual experience in the area of mathematics is to incorporate experiential-oriented mathematics sites currently on the Internet into the curriculum. An experiential-oriented site is one where the students become actively engaged in the mathematical simulation. This is in contrast to sites where the student is merely presented with data. Whereas these are not pure virtual field trips, teachers can still use them to create online experiences. One of the best sites in this category is MEGA MATH. This experiential site takes students into various mathematical concepts such as the following topic links:

- The Most Colorful Math of All
- Games on Graphs
- Untangling the Mathematics of Knots
- Algorithms and Ice Cream for All
- Machines that Eat Your Words
- Welcome to the Hotel Infinity
- A Usual Day at Unusual School

Each of these unusual topics contains an additional set of links for the study of each unit. These subtopics include the following:

- Activities
- Background information
- Big Ideas and Key Concepts

How to Integrate Virtual Field Trips into the Curriculum

- Evaluation
- For Further Study
- NCTM (National Council for the Teaching of Mathematics) Standards
- Prep and Materials
- Vocabulary

Each of these subtopics also contains a narrative and additional links explaining the particular information in greater detail. The material is presented in an interesting and innovative fashion as it strives to give the students an experience with mathematics. Teachers can easily incorporate these areas as a basis for personal virtual field trips.

Besides using the Internet to locate geometric figures in the world, as described in the opening anecdote, there are also experiential sites devoted to the study of geometry. One of these types of Internet locations is THE GEOMETRY CENTER. This site provides interesting experiential material such as the following:

Current Projects—what's hot at the Center
Interactive Web and Java Applications—math you can manipulate
Multimedia Documents—hypertext papers, preprints, forum
Geometry Reference Archive—graphic images, formulas
Downloadable Software—source, binaries, documentation
Video Productions—descriptions, clips, ordering info
Course Materials—lab materials, student work

These are just a few selected examples of experiential mathematical Internet sites and their potential for a mathematics virtual field trip. To see the full range of what is currently out there, teachers can use the normal channels for discovering virtual site material: search engines, general education sites, and subject-matter sites. Teachers' individual curricula and creativity determine how they can incorporate virtual field trips into the classroom.

The Arts

Integrating virtual field trips into the arts is almost as easy as integrating them into social studies or language arts. There are already a number of experiential arts-oriented Internet sites online, sites that provide students

with actual art experiences as if they were either in a museum or having a hands-on lesson. Locating them is relatively easy. Using them, teachers can develop excellent virtual experiences for their students in the areas of the visual arts, theater, and music and dance.

Visual Arts

The easiest type of visual art-related virtual field trip that teachers can create is a trip to a special exhibit in an art museum. In this type of activity, teachers collect links to paintings by famous artists or of a specific style. Teachers then let students take trips through the exhibits, viewing the various works.

Teachers can begin a virtual field trip of this sort with a visit to the Web site WORLD WIDE ARTS RESOURCES. At this site, teachers can search almost any category even remotely associated with the visual arts. The most valuable aspect of the site is the search index that teachers can use to locate Internet material concerning every major artist in the field today.

If teachers want to put together an exhibit on the famous twentieth century pop art painter Roy Lichtenstein, all they have to do is type in Lichtenstein into this artists search index. They would find a number of links that include numerous references to Lichtenstein's work:

Lichtenstein, Roy
painting, sculpture, pop, American, 20th century.

The Greatest Painters on the Web
Great artists on the web — from Leonardo to Lichtenstein, links featuring the best web sites on: Chagall, Dali, Durer, Gauguin, Kandinsky, Klee, Leonardo, Lichtenstein, Magritte, Michelangelo, Miro, Monet, Picasso, Rembrandt, Renoir, Turner, van Gogh, Warhol

Lichtenstein, Roy
Roy Lichtenstein Roy Lichtenstein born in 1923 in New York. In 1939-40 he studied under Reginald Marsh at the Art Students' League, New York, and 1940-43 and . . .

These links provide teachers with numerous reproductions of his paintings, along with biographical material and articles about his life and fairly recent death. It is surprisingly easy for teachers to integrate this material into a virtual field trip (see chapter 3). This search process on the WORLD WIDE ARTS RESOURCES site works for every artist imaginable.

SkyLight Professional Development

How to Integrate Virtual Field Trips into the Curriculum

Teachers can also integrate various art-oriented learning activities into the visual art virtual field trip. Teachers around the world have created a variety of sites that provide exceptional ideas and examples for everyday teachers. Teachers can find a collection of these types of sites using a general educational site such as TEACHERS HELPING TEACHERS or KATHY SCHROCK'S GUIDE TO EDUCATORS.

Theater

Virtual field trips in the area of theater take a little more work than those in the visual arts. In the first place, there is no one all-encompassing Web site in which to locate materials. Also, unlike looking at reproductions of artists' work, it is basically impossible to reproduce a full play or musical on the computer screen. Still, there are a number of avenues that a teacher, using some creativity, can pursue in constructing a virtual field trip for theater students.

Almost every Broadway and off-Broadway play has a number of Internet sites associated with it. These pages fall into two basic categories: official sites created by the producers and theaters themselves and sites established by the many fans of that particular show. Teachers can integrate these different sites into a virtual experience with a little searching and design.

Teachers can integrate material of this sort into both pure theater arts classes, as well as into the general curriculum. Imagine that a teacher is studying early twentieth century American culture and wants to incorporate the award-winning Broadway musical *Ragtime* (McNally et al. 1998) into a virtual class experience. The best place to commence the search for materials is with the use of the search engine METACRAWLER. By typing in the search term "Ragtime," the teacher receives approximately fifty examples, including the following links and descriptions:

Ragtime
This site is slowly, but surely, moving to www.journey-on.com/ragtime/ and becoming a tribute to the Los Angeles production and cast. I know that will . . . http://www.geocities.com/Broadway/Stage/4228/ (AltaVista)

Ragtime: The Musical
Click here to enter the Ragtime: The Musical Home Page. http://members. aol.com/km502/ragtime.htm (AltaVista)

SkyLight Professional Development

New York Times: The 1998 Tony Award Nominations
Nominees listed with related articles and reviews from the New York Times. Free registration required. http://www.nytimes.com/library/theater/tonys-list.html (Infoseek)

Great Performances: Creating Ragtime
- go behind-the-scenes and see the process of bringing "Ragtime" to a new Broadway theater constructed from two pre-existing 42nd Street landmark houses. http://www.pbs.org/wnet/gperf/ragtime/index.html (Yahoo!)

Ragtime
- The Immigrant Website. Unofficial site for the Broadway musical. http://www.gemonline.net/fordcenter (Yahoo!)

These sites bring together vast amounts of information about the musical, including a synopsis of the story line, the cast, the songs, and the history of the show, featuring information about its Tony Awards. Teachers can also locate lyrics and photos from the various productions of this show around the country. Teachers can then integrate all of this material into a theater-oriented virtual field trip.

Teachers can easily expand this particular activity using links to the dozens of Internet sites concerning ragtime music, many of which also came up in the METACRAWLER search. These sites contain vast amounts of information about the genre and its musicians, along with a large number of midi and other sound files, all of which contain examples of this particular style of music. Using these links, the teacher can develop a full curricular experience.

This is just one example of how teachers can construct virtual field trips in theater. As was outlined earlier with authors in the language arts section, teachers can construct virtual visits with famous playwrights and lyricists such as Stephen Sondheim and Andrew Lloyd Weber. With a little searching, teachers can also insert links on field trip sites that provide online scripts that students can work on together in cooperative groups. All teachers need to create an interesting Internet experience is a little creativity.

Music and Dance

Putting together a virtual field trip for music and dance curricula is quite possible, depending on the goals of the teacher. Although teachers can most likely find Internet sources of musical score sheets or instructions on how to dance a dance, this is not the best use of virtual field trip time—either in the construction of a trip or in the time that students would take to learn such material.

Teachers can easily use virtual field trips to supplement classroom lessons. A virtual field trip studying the composer Mozart provides information about his life, works, his historical time period, and the background of his career. Teachers can complement this trip with examples of his music on compact disk or cassette or by having the students experience a real field trip to hear a symphony orchestra performing works by Mozart.

This type of virtual field trip works with a dance curriculum as well. If students are studying the famous choreographer Merce Cunningham, teachers can locate substantial material on his work by searching his name on METACRAWLER. This search provides well over a dozen Internet sites, including the following all-encompassing links:

Merce Cunningham Dance
Excite: "There's no thinking involved in my choreography . . . I don't work through images or ideas ? I work through the body . . . If the dancer dances ? which is not the same as having theories about dancing or wishing to dance or trying to dance? everything is there. http://www.merce.org/home.html (AltaVista, Excite, Lycos)

Merce: Biography
Excite, WebCrawler: Merce Cunningham developed his own school of dancing and choreography, the continuity of which no longer relies on linear elements, be they narrative or psychological, nor does it rely on a movement towards and away from climax. http://www.merce.org/merce_bio.html (Excite, WebCrawler)

From these sites, teachers can provide students with Cunningham's history and background, information about his various dances and dancers in his troupe, and pictures of him and his dance company. Teachers can then supplement this material by showing videotaped examples of his work, taking a real field trip to see his work performed, or teaching examples of his choreography to students.

Although the arts are the most experiential of all of the curricular subjects, constructing virtual field trips in the visual arts, theater, or music and dance can still provide students with an enriched experience, especially when it is integrated with real experiences.

SkyLight Professional Development

READY-TO-USE TEACHER-CREATED VIRTUAL FIELD TRIPS

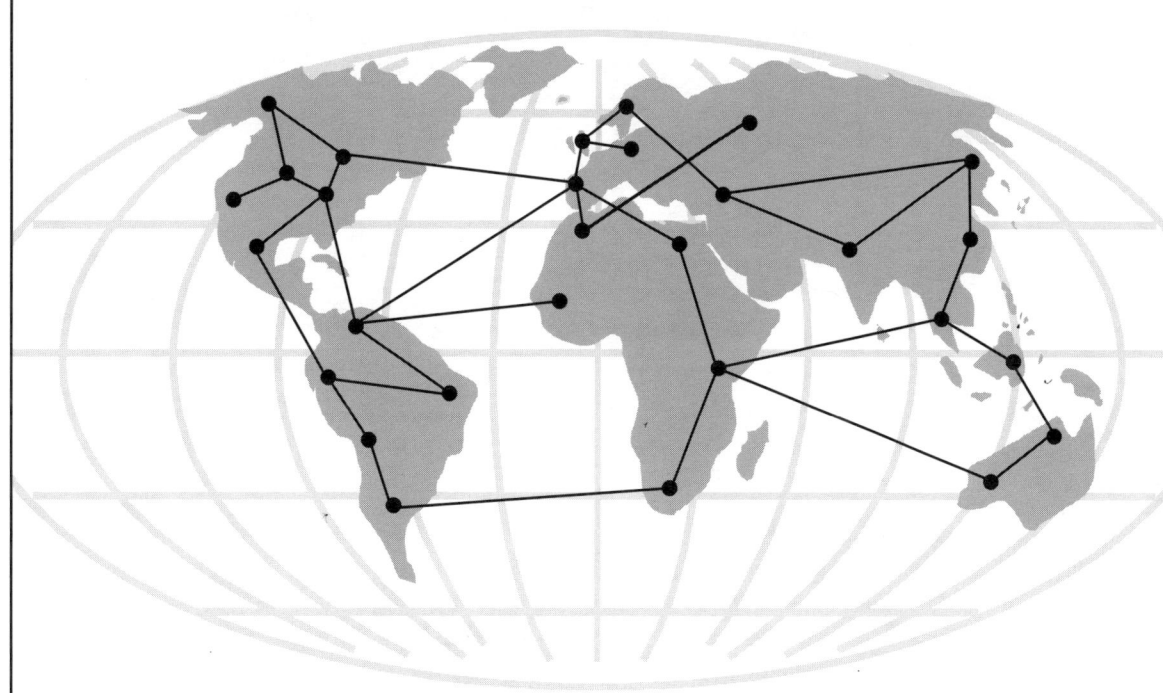

CHAPTER SIX

Ready-to-Use Teacher-Created Virtual Field Trips

CHAPTER 6

One primary goal of this book is to promote the practical application of virtual field trips into the average classroom teacher's curriculum. Although there are abundant examples and ideas provided throughout the previous chapters, actual models of this process by everyday classroom teachers are the best exemplification of this curricular exercise.

This chapter comprises a collection of lessons by current classroom teachers from around the country who regularly incorporate virtual field trips into their educational program (see Figure 6.1). These lessons are examples of how teachers are actually doing what this book promotes. Teachers can use the lessons as is, adapt them to their own particular curricula, or use them to spark ideas to create their own original virtual field trips.

The lessons are presented in a very basic, easy-to-use form. Each contains a short introduction, a list of materials required for the lesson, and a simple step-by-step activity, including a list of the Internet sites incorporated into the lesson. Teachers can find the mentioned Internet addresses directly in the lesson, rather than in the section of URLs in the back of the book. Please note that for the sake of brevity, the "http://" is removed from all URLs throughout

the chapter. The "www" is used for those addresses that originally had it.

Teacher Lesson Ideas		
TITLE	**TOPIC**	**GRADE RANGE**
A Trip to a Spider's Habitat	Science: *Biology*	K–3
A Trip Out of My Town	Social Studies: *Geography, History, Humanities*	4–12
A Trip in History to Visit Bleeding Kansas	Social Studies: *History*	5–12
A Trip to Medieval Times	Language Arts: *Literature* Social Studies: *History*	6–9
A Trip to See the Work of Diego Rivera	The Arts: *Visual Arts*	6–12
A Trip to a Weather Bureau	Mathematics: *Statistical Analysis* Science: *Geography*	7–12

Figure 6.1

It is crucial that all teachers develop a valid assessment for their particular teaching situation. Whereas teachers can use the activities in these lessons across many grade levels and in numerous teaching situations, teachers need to tailor assessment needs to students (see chapter 4). Some of the lessons in this chapter cover a grade range as broad as 4–12; the assessment strategies of the fourth grade teacher vary widely from that of the senior high teacher. Teachers need to keep this in mind as they incorporate the following lessons into their classrooms.

SkyLight Professional Development

A Trip to a Spider's Habitat

Submitted by
Addie Gaines
Seneca Elementary School
Seneca, MO

Amy Griffin
Crewe Primary School
Crewe, VA

Grade Range
  K-3

Topic Areas
  Science: Biology

Objective
  Two classes exchange e-mail and spider photos via the computer. Students use disposable cameras as spidercams to take the pictures. Teachers design a Web site to further exchange information about spiders, to publish learning activities that each class completes as a part of the spider unit, to share spider links that they visit, and to provide a spider photo gallery for students' future use.

  Visit this Web site at: www.geocities.com/Athens/Aegean/2221/spiderproject1.html

Materials
  - E-mail access
  - Disposable cameras
  - Scanner
  - Spiders to photograph
  - Server space (optional)

Activity
  1. Locate another classroom to cooperate with on this. To provide the greatest variety of data, try to pair your class with

lesson continued on next page

students from another part of the country. You can find teachers willing to participate on a joint project such as this through the use of the guest book on TEACHERS HELPING TEACHERS.

2. Schedule your unit studies for the same time period. This allows immediate contact between the students. (Be aware of differences in time zones.)

3. Use a variety of projects, literature, and Web sites for curricular information.

4. Use the following URL examples for research:

>**Spider Unit**
>www.geocities.com/Athens/Troy/5059/spider.html
>
>**I Love Spiders**
>www.geocities.com/Athens/Aegean/2221/spiders.html
>
>**Spiders Home Page**
>www.sedl.org/scimath/pasopartners/spiders/welcome.html
>
>**Spider Glider—Science Museum of Minnesota**
>www.sci.mus.mn.us/sln/tf/s/spiderglider/spiderglider.html
>
>**The Hobo Spider Web Site**
>www.srv.net/~dkv/hoboindx.html
>
>**You Can—Spider Webs**
>www.beakman.com/spider/spider.html
>
>**Arachnology—Kids**
>dns.ufsia.ac.be/Arachnology/Pages/Kids.html
>
>**Hey! A Brown Recluse Spider Bit Me!**
>kidshealth.org/kid/games/brown_recluse.html
>
>**Anansi WebSide Stories**
>www.anansi.org/webwalker/story1.htm
>
>**The Legend of the Christmas Spider**
>users.intercomm.com/greg/christmas/spider.html
>
>**Arachnology—Stories**
>dns.ufsia.ac.be/Arachnology/Pages/A_stories.html#story1

The Learning Circle's Halloween Spider Webs—Gryphon House Online
www.ghbooks.com/activity/10007135.htm

Thumbnails of Spiders in NW Europe
www.xs4all.nl/~harhiem/thumbnails spidhome_thumbnails.htm

5. Purchase disposable cameras and provide students with the opportunity to take spider photos.

6. Exchange the information and photos via e-mail. Scanners can easily translate photos into gifs that can be sent as attachments to the e-mail and later uploaded onto the classroom Web site. Print e-mails and photos.

7. Each class can create a display to share what they have learned with the rest of the school.

8. Create a shared Web site to display the photos and information for future access and sharing with other classrooms.

9. Teachers can easily adapt this project to other subjects within the science curriculum.

Assessment

Assessment varies depending on the particular objectives of the classroom curriculum and the material that is covered in other parts of the unit.

A Trip Out of My Town

Submitted by
Jarvis Kerr
Arizona Academy of Accelerated Academics
Winslow, AZ

Grade Range
  4-12

Topic Areas
  Social Studies: Geography, History, Humanities

Objective
  This trip provides students with an opportunity to visit locations outside of their town. This experience can take from one to two hours per day for approximately six weeks. It is similar to a live camping trip to an area that is unfamiliar to the camper. There are three parts to the project: preparation, the trip, and the report on what the traveler discovers. Some trailblazing for those students who may continue with the online experience can also be included with the lesson.

Materials
- Floppy disks
- A word processor program

Activity
1. URLs depend on the individual student's objective. However, there are some excellent Internet sites that all students can incorporate into their research. Visit the following URL; then visit with the cam owner by e-mail, if at all possible:

    Digital Cam Network
    www.dcn.com

    There are many different types of sites that students can visit, again, dependent on the objective of the exercise. If a student's objective is to visit a foreign country, the student can use the Department of State Web site to see travel restrictions (if any) and get a thumbnail sketch of the country. Overnight stays require students to search for a lodging URL. Try the following Web site for travel within the United States:

Mapquest
www.mapquest.com

Since this objective is research, have students hunt around a little. If they get stuck, they can ask us for some direction. Also encourage them to contact government bodies and individuals at their destination to get useful links and information.

2. *Planning:* Have students, individually or in teams, use word processors to list their objectives for visiting a destination. They would need to decide on several variables, including: the number traveling, living arrangements for fourteen days, costs, clothing (dependent on the weather at the site during that season), itinerary, subobjectives to be visited enroute, including departure and arrival information. Collect student plans, review, and return. The amount of detail required depends on the age of students. Obviously, the material required of a fourth grader would not be anywhere near as intensive as that required of a twelfth grader in this experience.

3. *Trip:* Have students log on to Internet and search for Web sites for their destination using YAHOO! The destination can be a city, such as "Houston," or a famous location, such as the "Statue of Liberty." When travelers arrive at their desired destination, they need to look around and see what they can find that is useful for meeting their principal objective. Have students use word processing programs to record the steps they used to arrive at their final destination. They should prepare a step-by-step URL trail for their classmates, recording side trips and data found along the way. These results can provide routes for other students to use to find data. For example, one team may be interested in geology while another may be interested in bridges or fishing. Students can share their data with teams that have the same interests, even if the final destinations of their trips differ.

Assessment

Students can present their data as news reports (given orally) to the class. The reports can include a list of the objectives and how they were achieved. In addition, they can create handouts detailing their experiences to share with the class or to put in a class scrapbook for future classes or parents to review.

A Trip in History to Visit Bleeding Kansas

Submitted by
Ginny Hoover
Abe Hubert Middle School
Garden City, KS

Grade Range
   5-12

Topic Areas
   Social Studies: History

Objective
   Take a trip to Kansas—back to the time when the nation was in the midst of its most devastating controversy. The North and the South were arguing about federalism, balance of power, slavery, and a number of trade issues—all of which was to soon explode into the Civil War. At the same time, more territories were desiring statehood. And one of those territories was Kansas.

Materials
   - The information sheet discussed below

Activity
   Use all of the following Internet sites in a virtual field trip activity. Put the following narrative onto an "itinerary" type of sheet for the students to direct themselves throughout the experience (see chapter 4).

   1. Visit the following site to see how the United States looked in the 1860s:

      Territorial Growth Map
      www.lib.utexas.edu/Libs/PCL/Map_collection/united_states/US_Terr_1860.jpg

   2. One controversy between the North and the South involved how new states would enter the Union. The South was very concerned about the balance of power—it was important to keep an equal amount of states on both sides of the issue. Would the next state be a slave state or a free state? Unfortunately, both Kansas and Nebraska were spotlighted in history because of this argument. Stephen Douglas, a Senator

from Illinois, was a powerful force in the Senate. He was a short, stocky man who gained lasting fame because of the Lincoln-Douglas debates. Visit the following site to learn more about the "Little Giant":

Stephen A. Douglas
www.pressenter.com/~douglas/douglas.html

3. Learn about the Lincoln-Douglas debates by visiting this site:

The Story of the Lincoln-Douglas Debates
gsbkmc.uchicago.edu/parker/museum97/lddbiog.html

4. Douglas backed a compromise called the Kansas-Nebraska Act. This act allowed slave states above the Missouri Compromise line. It also stated that the fate of these territories should be in the hands of the voters (popular sovereignty). See the Missouri Compromise line and learn more about the Kansas-Nebraska Act by visiting this site:

The Kansas Nebraska Act
usd316.k12.ks.us/GPMS/knact.htm

5. Now these two legal actions were in response to controlling the spread of slavery. Southerners wanted the right to spread to the west and north in the territories, while most Northerners wanted the spread of slavery stopped. The following site provides a slavery timeline:

A Slavery Timeline
www.amistad-thefilm.com/nonshock/movie/htmls/time_main.html

6. It was important to have a solid territorial government. Kansans gave it a try. See one effort made by a proslavery group:

Constitution Hall State Historic Site
history.cc.ukans.edu/heritage/kshs/places/constit.htm

7. Kansans had the right to vote on whether to be a slave state or a free state. But who would vote? The New England Emigrant Aid Society recruited settlers for Kansas who op-

lesson continued on next page

posed slavery and said Kansas should be free soil. The guns sent to Kansas from New England were called Beecher's Bibles. The following sites explain more about the Emigrant Aid Society and provide some primary documents:

The Massachusetts Emigrant Aid Society
xroads.virginia.edu/~hyper/hns/kansas/meas1.html

Kansas Collection Books
kuhttp.cc.ukans.edu/carrie/kancoll/books/emig_aid/emigrant.htm

8. Violence struck at Lawrence, Kansas. A federal marshal named J. B. Donaldson lead a large group of men into the city. They tore down and burned much of Lawrence. No one died, but it made a statement for slavery:

Kansas Territory: Crucible of American Experience
xroads.virginia.edu/~hyper/hns/kansas/kansas.html

9. John Brown believed that slavery was wrong. He took a more violent path. His strike against slavery included five deaths at Potawatomie, KS. Read about his strikes in Kansas:

John Brown and the Valley of the Shadow
jefferson.village.virginia.edu/jbrown/master.html

10. Kansas struggles to become a state. Proslavery was winning the battle, but "free soilers" would not accept defeat. For a while, Kansas had two capitals. The two sides continued to battle. Jayhawkers became a name used for Kansans who fought to keep slavery from Kansas. Bushwackers became the nickname used for people fighting to allow slavery in Kansas. This name continued into the Civil War and was used as a name for Confederate guerrillas:

The Origin of the Name Jayhawkers
www4.pair.com/justfolk/CWPG8.HTM

The History of the Jayhawk Bushwackers
www.jayhawks.org/trad/jhawkhistory.html

William Quantrill and the Lawrence Massacre
xroads.virginia.edu/~HYPER/CONTEXTS/Kansas/quantril.html

Quantrill's Flag
www.ukans.edu/heritage/kshs/places/coolquan.htm

11. Stop by this site to learn about one of the last conflicts between proslavery and free soilers:

    Marais des Cygnes State Historical Site
    history.cc.ukans.edu/heritage/kshs/places/marahist.htm

12. Finally, Kansas becomes a free state. Now, this is after maintaining two capitals with two opposing political ideas causing a bloody conflict. That is why this period is called Bleeding Kansas. Some people would argue that the Civil War started in Kansas. It would appear that unofficially it did. What do you think?

13. Kansas becomes a state. Shortly after, the United States became involved in an internal war: the North against the South. It is sometimes called the War Between the States but most often the Civil War:

    Statehood to 1900
    raven.cc.ukans.edu/heritage/kshs/perspect/stat1900.htm

14. This is the new capitol of Kansas:

    The Capitols of Kansas
    www.fn.net/~howell/history/capital.html

    The Kansas Capitol
    www.ink.org/public/governor/pics/capitol.html

15. These are the symbols of Kansas:

    Kansas State Symbols
    www.paola-online.net/kansas.htm

16. Notice that your trip did not include stops at the Smithsonian, Library of Congress, and other outstanding sources in Washington, D.C. that have excellent Internet sites. It would be a good idea now for you to search those sites and find the pictures, diaries, letters, legal documents, and other primary sources available. Make that trip now.

lesson continued on next page

Assessment

Have students write a short answer response explaining why they agree or disagree with the following statement: The Civil War started in Kansas. To defend their positions, have students include references from at least three Web sites.

A Trip to Medieval Times

Submitted by
Steve Jacobson
La Mesa Junior High School
Santa Clarita, CA

Grade Range
  6-9

Topic Areas
  Language Arts: Literature
  Social Studies: History

Objective
  Use this lesson to prepare students for reading the novel *Catherine, Called Birdy* by Karen Cushman. In this lesson, students research life in Medieval times and gain an understanding of Medieval customs, beliefs, people, foods, and lifestyles. This lesson also works for any other novel or short story set within this time period.

Materials
- Writing materials
- Materials for costumes, visual aids, and artwork, as needed

Activity
1. Introduce the novel, *Catherine, Called Birdy*, to students. Explain that it takes place during the years 1290-1291. Let students know that they are going to research an aspect of Medieval life and present it to the class to gain a better understanding of life in those days.
2. Place students into cooperative groups of four or five.
3. Assign each group a broad topic heading from the following list:

    village life
    customs
    religions and beliefs
    food and drink
    royalty
    professions

lesson continued on next page

VIRTUAL FIELD TRIPS IN THE CYBERAGE

4. Give students time to research the different aspects of Medieval life and report on what they find to the class. Encourage them to use the following Internet sites for the information:

> **Medieval Domestic Life**
> www.millersv.edu/~english/homepage/duncan/medfem/domestic.html
>
> **Ravensgard Medieval Homepage**
> users.aol.com/gerekr/medieval.html
>
> **LBMS - The Middle Ages**
> schools.ci.burbank.ca.us/~luther/midages/beginhere.html

Assessment

Presentations in the form of skits, informative reports, or demonstrations.

A Trip to See the Work of Diego Rivera

Submitted by
B. J. Berquist
Loysville Youth Development Center
Loysville, PA

Grade Range
6-12

Topic Areas
The Arts: Visual Arts

Objective
Rivera believed that art should be available to the masses and not shut away in museums. He is one of the first graffiti wall artists. This trip exposes students to the work of this urban artist. It also encourages students to see art as a form of communication.

Materials
- Color print of at least part of the artwork done by Rivera on the Detroit Institute of Arts walls

Activity
1. Discuss the following with students: Art is a form of communication. Artists choose what and how they want to communicate. The time period influences artists' choices of what to communicate. Rivera portrays in this work political ideology, clothing styles, and social norms of the time.

2. Ask students to determine under what influences Rivera was working. By taking a virtual field trip to sites like the one cited below, students can see what a production line at the Ford Motor Company looked like, what the workers were wearing, how Rivera constructed his mural. Use the following Internet site:

   Diego Rivera at the DIA
   www.diamondial.org/rivera/

In 1932 Diego Rivera painted twenty-seven fresco panels titled Detroit Institute of Arts. These photographs show

lesson continued on next page

Diego Rivera and Frida Kahlo in the DIA as well as views taken at the Ford Motor Company River Rouge Plant, which served as a model for many aspects of the frescos.

3. Students can obtain additional images of production lines, laborers, clothing, people, and architecture from this period at The American Memory Internet site:

   American Memory / Library of Congress
   lcweb2.loc.gov/ammem/amhometxt.html

4. If students do not have access to the Internet, take the virtual field trips and share the researched material with students.

Assessment
Have students create a mural (on paper) that communicates an idea, style, or social norm of today.

A Trip to a Weather Bureau

Submitted by
   Robert Schuck
   Pacoima Middle School
   Los Angeles, CA

Grade Range
   7-12

Topic Areas
   Mathematics: Statistical Analysis
   Science: Geography

Objective
   In this lesson, students learn how to measure and collect data concerning local weather conditions, including temperature, wind, humidity, rain, and barometric pressure. They learn how to convert the collected data into measures of central tendency and pertinent percentages (involving fractions and decimals). They also learn how to analyze statistical findings to predict local weather trends and present their data using graphs and charts of statistical data.

Materials
- Materials to make weather instruments as presented at the Franklin Institute Science Museum Web site
- 28" X 36" one inch square graphing paper
- 28" X 36" blank chart paper
- Colored markers, pencils, rulers, yardsticks to make charts and graphs
- Optional: calculators

Activity
1. Discuss the following with the students: What is weather? How do we record it?
2. With students, visit the following Internet site and point out examples of weather forecasting:

lesson continued on next page

VIRTUAL FIELD TRIPS IN THE CYBERAGE

Weather Information Superhighway—United States National Weather Bureau
www.nws.fsu.edu/wxhwy.html

3. Have the students construct their own weather data collecting instruments. Encourage them to use the following Web site:

Franklin Institute Science Museum
sln.fi.edu/tfi/welcome.html

Click on the online exhibit titled "Franklin's Forecast, an online exhibit about weather forecasting." Scroll down to "make your own weather station." Have students, individually or in groups, make their own weather instruments, using the online directions.

4. Have students use their homemade weather data collecting instruments to collect and record weather data for at least ten days. The longer, the better.

5. After the collection period, have students analyze their data with Measures of Central Tendency.

Assessment

Have students' present their findings with visual aids of data. Students can give oral reports along with written reports.

Appendix A

A Virtual Field Trip Checklist

Use this checklist as you go through the process of creating your own virtual field trip. Either check them off or go over them in your head.

Title of Virtual Field Trip: _____

I. Determine Your Goals and Parameters
    Set Goals
        Why am I planning this specific trip?
        What curricular material will this trip cover?
        How will this experience enhance the students' learning in this unit?
    Outline the Scope of the Trip
        How much of the unit should I cover in this particular learning activity?
        Is the field trip going to be the major supplier of curricular information, or is it going to be a side experience solely meant to supplement material previously discussed?
        What student assessment can I use for the field trip?

II. Brainstorm a Model
    Create the Initial Web of Possibilities
        Include all of the goals
        Brainstorm possible activities for the goals
    Check for Viability
        Do the activities match the goals?
        Do I have to change the goals or activities?

continued on next page

SkyLight Professional Development

Check for Practicality
> Are the time limits sufficient?
> Is the student level appropriate?
> Are there available resources?

III. Investigate
Look for Existing Virtual Field Trip Sites
> Use METACRAWLER
> If none appropriate exist, plan for creation of personal field trip

Use Search Engines to Find Material
> Use METACRAWLER
> Use YAHOO! if appropriate

Search Educational Sites for Additional Material
> Use general education sites such as TEACHERS HELPING TEACHERS or KATHY SCHROCK'S GUIDE FOR EDUCATORS
> Use subject matter sites
> Use teacher guest books

IV. Make Decisions About Activities
Redo the Original Web of Possibilities
> Remove discarded goals and activities
> Add new goals and activities
> Add all titles and URLs of discovered Internet sites

Analyze the Appropriateness of the Collected Sites
> Check the appropriateness of the subject matter contained within the site
> Check the language level that is incorporated throughout the material
> Check the physical loading of the site—time to download

Reevaluate the Goals and Activities
> Recheck the goals of the virtual field trip:
> Do the Internet sites collected still cover the original goals of the experience?

continued on next page

Appendix A

>> Are there new goals to add, based on unexpected material that was discovered?
>> Are there goals that are no longer appropriate or feasible based on the sites that were or were not found?
> Recheck the activities of the virtual field trip:
>> Are there sufficient URLs for students to visit for each activity that is planned?
>> If not, is there time or desire to continue the search for additional sites, or should the proposed activity be dropped from the Internet session?
>> Do some of the sites collected suggest additional activities that should now be added to the virtual field trip?
> Recheck the time frame of the virtual field trip:
>> Is the original anticipated time frame sufficient for using all of the Web sites?
>> Does the time frame need to be adjusted up or down?
>> Do sites need to be deleted or added in adjustment to the time scheduled for the online experience?

V. Make a Logical Plan for Implementation into the Curriculum
> Create the trip structure
>> Conduct the trip together as an entire class, using one overhead-projected computer or a set of computers controlled by one central work station?
>> Let students conduct the trip on an individualized basis in a computer lab or at a classroom computer station where students can make their own decisions of which sites to visit and when to visit them?
>> Have students conduct the trip as an outside-the-classroom experience on a home, library, or community computer?
> Set time limits
>> Which Internet sites are mandatory for all students to visit?
>> Which URLs are optional?

continued on next page

Provide URL Access
- Create an itinerary for the trip?
- Provide students with a comprehensive list of URLs to investigate, divided by subject matter?
- Bookmark all of the potential sites on the classroom computer?
- Create an original Web site, or a page on a school site, that takes students along the virtual field trip, link by link?

Integrate Within the Curricular Unit
- Learning activities before the trip
- Learning activities after the trip
- Learning activities not covered by the trip
- Learning activities now covered by the trip

Check for Use of the Multiple Intelligences Theory
- Verbal/Linguistic
- Logical/Mathematical
- Visual/Spatial
- Bodily/Kinesthetic
- Musical/Rhythmic
- Interpersonal
- Intrapersonal
- Naturalist

VI. Address Assessment

VII. What Other Classes in the School Can Participate in this Virtual Field Trip?

Appendix B

Glossary

address. The location of a site on the Internet, usually beginning with "http://www." or just "www."; also referred to as the "URL" of the site.

bodily/kinesthetic intelligence. The ability to use one's whole body to express ideas and feelings and use one's hands to produce or transform things (Armstrong 1994).

bookmark. A favorite site that teachers can place in a special menu on a browser, enabling teachers to instantaneously link to the site by simply selecting the name.

browser. Software that allows people to work on the Internet.

cache. The special memory that the browser uses to remember frequently visited sites; it is meant to significantly reduce download times on sites previously visited.

chat channel/room. A specific channel on the Internet Relay Chat (IRC), usually dedicated to a particular topic or interest; a chat room operates in the same fashion but is generally part of a private Web site or feature of an Internet provider.

cyberage. A word for the modern age, in which the information services processed electronically, or on-line, is central to the function of society.

cyber-experience. A learning activity on the Internet.

cyberphobia. A fear or a general uncomfortable feeling toward anything connected to the Internet and online processes.

cyberspace. A word used to describe the expansiveness of the Internet and online services.

directory. A site that lists other Internet sites by category—similar in function to a search engine.

download. When someone takes a program or information off of the Internet and places it onto a personal computer or printer.

e-mail. Mail messages sent electronically from one computer to another; an e-mail address contains the person's user name, the @ sign, and then the server name.

gif. Graphics on the Internet are called gifs. Conversion is either done through a graphic conversion program or automatically by the scanner or Web site creation program.

graphic. The term for pictures or artistic word designs that are used on the Internet.

guest books. Sections of home pages where people can leave messages for other users to read and respond.

home page. An Internet site dedicated to a topic or a personal interest; home pages are the format individuals and businesses use to promote their interests on the Internet; home pages often contain links to other home pages, usually of the same interest.

html. The programming language that is used in Web sites on the Internet to transform text and formats into what is seen online; most new home-page–creation software programs do not require the user to know html, they simply convert it for the user.

Internet. The overall term used to describe the global system of networked computers that allow the transfer of information and communication between users; in this book, it also refers to all online services: the World Wide Web, telnet, newsgroups, and e-mail services and systems.

Internet Relay Chat (IRC). A separate system from the World Wide Web in which users can talk to each other in real time by typing their messages onto their keyboard and receiving an immediate response from others on the same channel.

interpersonal intelligence. The ability to perceive and make distinctions in the moods, intentions, motivations, and feelings of other people (Armstrong 1994).

intrapersonal intelligence. The ability to be self-aware and to act adaptively on the basis of that knowledge (Armstrong 1994).

Integrated Service Digital Network (ISDN) link. A very fast Internet line; significantly faster connection speed than convention modems (i.e., 56k).

link. Specially colored words, phrases, or graphics on Internet sites that when clicked on, or selected, provide a direct connection from one Internet site to another.

logical/mathematical intelligence. The capacity to use numbers effectively and to reason well (Armstrong 1994).

multiple intelligences. Howard Gardner's theory that defines eight intelligences: verbal/linguistic, musical/rhythmic, logical/mathematical, interpersonal, intrapersonal, bodily/kinesthetic, naturalist.

musical/rhythmic intelligence. The capacity to perceive, discriminate, transform, and express musical forms (Armstrong 1994).

naturalist intelligence. The ability to categorize and classify elements in the ecosystem (Fogarty 1997).

networking. People connecting with others who share the same interests, via the Internet or the IRC.

packaged field trips. A field trip that has been prepared for the teacher; trip without any significant feedback by those who will use it.

personalized field trips. A field trip that a teacher designs to address the curriculum of those who will use it.

search engine. A directory assistance for the Internet that allows a user to locate sites whose titles or descriptions contain specific search words.

site. Another name for a home page location on the Internet.

Uniform Resource Location (URL). The official location spot for a site on the Internet; also known as an address.

upload. The process of putting information on the Internet from a computer, such as onto one's own home page.

SkyLight Professional Development

verbal/linguistic intelligence. The capacity to use words effectively, whether orally or in writing (Armstrong 1994).

virtual field trip. A learning activity on the Internet, in which an experience is simulated as if it was actually experienced by the student.

visual/spatial intelligence. The ability to perceive the visual-spatial world accurately and to perform transformations upon those perceptions (Armstrong 1994).

Web site. Another name for a home page; the information someone or some company places at a particular URL.

World Wide Web. The part of the Internet that contains home pages or Web sites. A formal World Wide Web listing includes the letters www. in the URL.

Appendix C
Index of URLs

ADVENTURE ONLINE
http://www.adventureonline.com

AN AMAZON ADVENTURE
http://jajhs.kana.k12.wv.us/amazo/index.htm

THE AMERICAN CIVIL WAR HOMEPAGE
http://sunsite.utk.edu/civil-war

THE ANCIENT EGYPTIAN CULTURE EXHIBIT
http://EMuseum.mankato.msus.edu/egypt

THE ART TEACHER CONNECTION
http://www.primenet.com/~arted

AUDIO ONLINE: STREAMED AUDIO FILES, MEDIA RESOURCES CENTER, UCB
http://www.lib.berkeley.edu/MRC/audiofiles.html

BYZANTINE RELIGIOUS ICONOGRAPHY AND ICON ART
http://www.csg-i.com/icons

THE CHILDREN'S LITERATURE WEB SITE
http://www.ucalgary.ca/~dkbrown/index.html

CNN INTERACTIVE
http://cnn.com/ALLPOLITICS

CODY'S SCIENCE EDUCATION ZONE!
http://ousdmail.ousd.k12.ca.us/~codypren/CSEZ_Home.htm

DESERT LIFE IN THE AMERICAN SOUTHWEST
http://www.desertusa.com/life.html

EXPLORATORIUM
http://www.exploratorium.edu/exploring/index.html

SkyLight Professional Development

FRANKLIN INSTITUTE SCIENCE MUSEUM
http://sln.fi.edu/tfi/welcome.html

THE GEOMETRY CENTER
http://www.geom.umn.edu

HAWAIIAN VOLCANO OBSERVATORY
http://wwwhvo.wr.usgs.gov/hazards

HISTORICAL TEXT ARCHIVE
http://www.msstate.edu/Archives/History/USA/usa.html

HISTORY/SOCIAL STUDIES WEB SITE FOR K-12 TEACHERS
http://www.execpc.com/~dboals/boals.html

IMAGINE HAWAII
http://imagine-hawaii.com

INFOSEEK
http://www.infoseek.com

INTERACTIVE MATHEMATICS ONLINE
http://tqd.advanced.org/2647/main.htm

THE JEFFERSON PROJECT
http://www.capweb.net/classic/jefferson/

JUDY BLUME'S OFFICIAL WEB SITE
http://www.judyblume.com

KATHY SCHROCK'S GUIDE FOR EDUCATORS
http://discoveryschool.com/schrockguide

LYCOS
http://www.lycos.com

THE MATH FORUM HOME PAGE
http://forum.swarthmore.edu

MEGA MATH
http://www.c3.lanl.gov/mega-math/menu.html

METACRAWLER
http://www.go2net.com/search.html

Appendix C

THE NAPOLEON SERIES: LIFE & TIMES OF NAPOLEON BONEPARTE
http://www.ping.be/napoleon.series

NASA
http://www.nasa.gov

A PAGE OF INFORMATION ON ELEPHANTS
http://www.inactive.demon.co.uk/elephant.html

REMEMBER THE MAINE
http://www.smithsonianmag.si.edu/smithsonian/issues98/feb98/maine.html

ROBERT FROST: THREE VOLUMES AND C.
http://www.columbia.edu/acis/bartleby/frost

SMITHSONIAN INSTITUTE
http://www.si.edu

A TEACHER'S GUIDE TO THE HOLOCAUST
http://fcit.coedu.usf.edu/Holocaust

TEACHERS HELPING TEACHERS
http://www.pacificnet.net/~mandel

TIGER INFORMATION CENTER
http://5tigers.org

USA TODAY WEATHER—A TYPICAL NORTHERN HEMISPHERE HURRICANE
http://www.usatoday.com/weather/tg/whurwhat/whurwhat.htm

THE VIRTUAL FIELD TRIPS SITE
http://www.field-guides.com

A VIRTUAL GEOLOGICAL FIELD TRIP TO ICELAND
http://www.casdn.neu.edu/~geology/department/staff/colgan/iceland/welcome.htm

WORLD WIDE ARTS RESOURCES
http://wwar.com

YAHOO!
http://www.yahoo.com

SkyLight Professional Development

References

Armstrong, T. 1994. *Multiple intelligences in the classroom.* Alexandria, VA: Association for Supervision and Curriculum Development.

Bigham, V. 1998. *Online education resources.* Englewood Cliffs, N.J: Prentice-Hall.

Buettner, D., and C. deMoll. 1996. Journey into the unknown. *Learning* 24(4): 36–38.

Checkley, K. 1997. The first seven...and the eighth. *Educational Leadership* 55(1): 8-13.

Cushman, K. 1994. *Catherine, called Birdy.* New York: HarperCollins Publishers, Inc.

Drier, H. S., K. M. Dawson, and J. Garofalo. 1999. Not your typical math class. *Educational Leadership* 56(5): 21–25.

Eisner, E. 1979. *The educational imagination.* New York: Macmillan Publishing.

Fogarty, R. 1997. *Problem-based learning and other curriculum models.* Arlington Heights, IL: IRI/SkyLight Training and Publishing, Inc.

Gardner, H. 1993. *Multiple intelligences: The theory in practice.* New York: BasicBooks.

Giagnocano, G. 1996. *Educator's internet companion.* Classroom Connect.

Goldsworthy, R. 1997. Real-world field trips. *Learning and leading with technology* 24(7): 26–29.

Joyce, B., and M. Weil. 1996. *Models of teaching* 5th ed. Boston: Allyn and Bacon.

Kipling, R. 1894. *The jungle book.* (Original published date).

Krepel, W.J., and C.R. Duvall. 1981. *Field trips: A guide for planning and conducting educational experiences.* Washington, D.C.: National Education Association.

Latham, A. 1999. Computers and achievement. *Educational Leadership* 56(5): 87–88.

Lee, H. 1960. *To kill a mockingbird.* Philadelphia: Lippincott.

Maclachlan, P. 1985. *Sarah plain and tall.* New York: Harper & Row.

McNally, T., S. Flaherty, and L. Ahrens. 1998. *Ragtime—the musical.* Livent (U.S.) Inc.

Mandel, S.M. 1998. *Social studies in the cyberage: Applications with cooperative learning.* Arlington Heights, IL: Skylight Training and Publishing Inc.

Mandel, S.M. 1991. *Responses to cooperative learning processes among elementary-age students.* ERIC Clearinghouse on Elementary and Early Childhood Education, ED 332808.

Millan, D.A. 1995. Field trips: Maximizing the experience. In *Experience and the curriculum.* Kendall/Hunt Publishing Company: Dubuque, Iowa.

Miller, A. 1953. *The crucible.* New York: Viking Press.

O'Dell, S. 1990. *Island of the blue dolphin.* Boston: Houghton Mifflin.

Rudman, C.L. 1994. A review of the use and implementation of science field trips. *School science and mathematics* 94(3): 138–141.

Slavin, R.E. 1990. *Cooperative learning: Theory, research, and practice.* Englewood Cliffs, NJ: Prentice-Hall.

Tapscott, D. 1999. Educating the net generation. *Educational Leadership* 56(5): 6–11.

Thomas, L., and D. Knezek. 1999. National educational technology standards. *Educational Leadership* 56(5): 27.

Index

Abbington Village (Web site), 111
Academic Info: U.S. History Home Page & Index (Web site), 30
Activities, learning
    after the trip, 62, 97–98
    before the trip, 62, 97
    not covered by the trip, 62, 98
    that trip will now cover, 62, 99
Activities for virtual field trip
    choosing, 54–55
    determining, 152–53
    reevaluating, 58–59, 91–93
Advanced Placement U.S. History Syllabus (Web site), 30
Advantages of virtual field trips, 7–20
Adventure Online (Web site), 47
AltaVista (search engine), 54, 80, 81, 127, 129
Amazon Adventure, An (Web site), 9
American Civil War Ethnography—Home (Web site), 52
American Civil War Homepage, The (Web site), 32, 52
American History Sources for Students (Web site), 30
"American Invention," An, (Web site), 122
American Memory/Library of Congress (Web site), 53, *55*, 148
Analyzing Web sites, 55–58, 87–91
Anansi WebSide Stories (Web site), 136
Ancient Egyptian Culture Exhibit (Web site), 116
Appropriateness of Web site material, 56
Arachnology—Kids (Web site), 136

Arachnology—Stories (Web site), 136
Aristotle, 14
Arizona Academy of Accelerated Academics (Winslow, AZ), 138
Arthur Miller's *The Crucible:* Fact & Fiction (Web site), 35
Arts curriculum, using virtual field trips in, 125–29
Art Teacher Connection, The (Web site), 32
Ask Dr. Math—Archives (Web site), 12
Assessment of virtual field trip, 44, 64–66, 74, 99–102
Audio Online: Streamed Audio Files, Media Resources Center, UCB (Web site), 116
Audio Recordings of Shakespeare (Web site), 81, *82*
!Australian wildlife! Rain forest birds, mammals, reptiles, . . . (Web site), 49

Berquist, B. J., 147
Better That Witches Should Live (Web site), 32
Biological Web sites, 121
BioPoint (Web site), 122
Bleeding Kansas, virtual field trip to, *134*, 140–44
Blume, Judy, 112
Bodily/kinesthetic intelligence, 64, *100*
Boston Tea Party, virtual field trip to, 39–41
Bradbury, Mary, 28
Brainstorming a model for a virtual field trip, 44–47, 75–79, 151–52

SkyLight Professional Development

Brown, John, 142
Byzantine Empire, virtual field trip on, 116
Byzantine Religious Iconography and Icon Art (Web site), 116

Capitols of Kansas, The (Web site), 143
Castles on the Web (Web site), 83, *85, 89, 90,* 94
Catherine, Called Birdy (Cushman), 145
Chagall, Marc, 126
Charles IV, King, 106
Checklist, virtual field trip, 66–67, 151–54
Chicago Cultural Center (Web site), 106
Children's Literature Web Guide (Web site), 112
Children's Literature Web Site, The, 31
Chocolate in the Forest (Web site), 122
Chocolate Invades Europe (Web site), 122
Cinco de Mayo (Web site), 119
Cinco de Mayo, virtual field trip on, 118–19
Cinco de Mayo Fiesta Official Site (Web site), 119
Civil rights, virtual field trip on, 116
Civil War Cookbook (Web site), *55*
Civil War Interactive (Web site), 52
Civil War Years, (Web site), *55*
CNN Interactive (Web site), 36, 119, 120
Cody's Science Education Zone! (Web site), 31
Commercial Web sites, 18, 47
Community, planning a virtual field trip to a, 114
Conducting the virtual field trip, 95–99
Constitution Hall State Historic Site (Web site), 141
Crewe Primary School (Crewe, VA), 135
Critical-thinking problems, using Internet to create, 123–24
Crossing the Frontier (Web site), 109

Crucible, The, planning a virtual field trip on, 26–35
Cunningham, Merce, 129
Current events, virtual field trip for studying, 119–20
Curricular material
    accessing via Internet, 11–13
    trip will cover, determining what, 43
Curriculum
    integrating virtual field trips into, 105–29, 153–54
    Internet and, 11
Cushman, Karen, 145
Cyberspace Museum of Natural History and Exploration Technology, The (Web site), 20

Dali, Salvador, 126
Dance, virtual field trip for studying, 128–29
da Vinci, Leonardo, 126
Democracy, virtual field trip for studying, 117–18
Derby Square Tours (Web site), 28
Desert Life in the American Southwest (Web site), 8
Detroit Institute of Arts, 147
Diego Rivera at the DIA (Web site), 147
Digital Cam Network (Web site), 138
Directories, 27. *See also* Yahoo!; Search engines
Directory versus search engine, 28
Discussion from Town Crier, including bibliography (Web site), 33
Donaldson, J. B., 142
Douglas, Stephen, 140
Durer, Albrecht, 126

Earthforce (Web site), 121
Easty, Mary, 28
Education Web sites, 29–30, 83
    packaged virtual field trips and, 18–19
    searching, 52

SkyLight Professional Development

Index

Egypt, ancient, virtual field trip on, 116
Eiffel Tower@ (Web site), 106
Electronic bulletin boards. *See* Teacher guest books
Elephants, A Page of Information on (Web site), 18
Excite (search engine), 51, 54, 80, 113, 119, 129
Exhibits Collection—The Middle Ages (Web site), 84, *85, 89, 90,* 94
Existing virtual field trip sites, locating, 47–50
Experiential Mathematical Web sites, 124–25
Exploratorium (Web site), 122
Explore New England (Web site), 111
Exploring Hair: "Better Hair Through Chemistry" (Web site), 122
Exploring Memories: "Young in Mind" (Web site), 122

"Feel Good" Food (Web site), 122
Field trips
    as curricular enhancement, 13–14
    definition of, 14
    educational value of, 14–15
    factors that contribute to success of, 15
    virtual versus real-life, 16–18
Flights of Inspiration (Web site), 121
Folger Shakespeare Library, The (Web site), 80, *82*
Ford Motor Company, 147, 148
Franklin Institute Science Museum (Web site), 121, 149, 150
Franklin's Forecast (Web site), 121
From Bean to Bar (Web site), 122
Frost, Robert, 12, 110–11

Gaines, Addie, 135
Gallery of the Open Frontier (Web site), 109
Gardner, Howard, 62, 65

Gauguin, Paul, 126
GeoCities—RainForest (Web site), 49
Geographical Web sites, 121
Geological Web sites, 121
Geometry Center, The (Web site), 32, 125
Getty, The (Web site), 114
Getty Center, The, 114
Gettysburg, Battle of, virtual field trip, 51–*55*
Gettysburg Address (Web site), *55*
Goals of virtual field trip
    determining, 73–74, 151
    reevaluating, 58–59, 91–92
    setting, 41–43
Greatest Painters on the Web, The (Web site), 126
Great Performances: Creating Ragtime (Web site), 128
Great Pyramid (Web site), 106
Griffin, Amy, 135

Hannibal, Missouri (Web site), 110
Hawaiian Volcano Observatory (Web site), 8
Health Help or Risk (Web site), 122
Hey! A Brown Recluse Spider Bit Me! (Web site), 136
Historical Text Archive (Web site), 12, 33, 115
History curriculum, using virtual field trips in, 113–16
History of Costume (Web site), 84
History of the Jayhawk Bushwackers, The (Web site), 142
History/Social Studies Web Site for K–12 Teachers, 24, 31, 52, 83–84, 109, 115, 116
Hobo Spider Web Site, The, 136
Holocaust, virtual field trip on, 116
Hoover, Ginny, 140
Hubert, Abe, Middle School (Garden City, KS), 140

SkyLight Professional Development

Humanities curriculum, using virtual field trips in, 117–20
Hyperlink, 95

Iceland, A Virtual Geological Field Trip to (Web site), 19
I Love Spiders (Web site), 136
Imagine Hawaii (Web site), 18
Implementing
    virtual field trip, 95–99
    virtual field trip into the curriculum, 59–62, 105–29, 153–54
Independence Hall@ (Web site), 106
Information, accessing previously unattainable, 10–11
Informational sites and packaged virtual field trips, 18
Infoseek (search engine), 20, 24, 25, 26, 27, 28, 54, 79, 80, 81, 113, 114
Infoseek: Cinco de Mayo (Web site), 119
Integrating virtual field trips into curriculum, 59–62, 105–29, 153–54
Interactive Mathematics Online (Web site), 124
Internet. *See also* Web site(s)
    activities, usefulness of, 123
    convenience of, 10
    as an educational resourc, 9–13
    Projects for Algebra (Web site), 13
    search engines, 25–27
    Shakespeare resources (Web site), 80, *82*
    sites, investigating, 47–54
    sites, locating, 24
Interpersonal intelligence, 64, *100*
Interviews, using Internet to conduct, 123
Investigating Internet sites for virtual field trip, 47–54
Irwin, Robert, 114
Island of the Blue Dolphin (O'Dell), 108

Jacobson, Steve, 145
Jason Project, The (Web site), 20
Jefferson, Thomas, 106
Jefferson Project (Web site), 117
John Brown and the Valley of the Shadow (Web site), 142
Joy of Concrete, The (Web site), 106
Judy Blume's Official Web Site, 112
Julius Caesar, 72
Jungle Book, The (Kipling), 113

Kahlo, Frida, 148
Kandinsky, Wassily, 126
Kansas, bleeding, virtual field trip to, *134*, 140–44
Kansas Capitol, The (Web site), 143
Kansas Collection Books (Web site), 142
Kansas-Nebraska Act, The (Web site), 141
Kansas State Symbols (Web site), 143
Kansas Territory: Crucible of American Experience, 142
Kathy Schrock's Guide for Educators (Web site), 29, 52, 54, 83, 127, 152
Kerr, Jarvis, 138
Kipling, Rudyard, 113
Klee, Paul, 126

La Mesa Junior High School (Santa Clarita, CA), 145
Language arts curriculum, using virtual field trips in, 108–13
Language Arts Cyberguides (Web site), 30
LBMS—The Middle Ages (Web site), 84, *85*, *89*, *90*, 91, 146
Learning Circle's Halloween Spider Webs—Gryphon House Online (Web site), 137
Lee, Harper, 108
Legend of the Christmas Spider, The (Web site), 136
Lesson ideas for ready-made virtual field trips, *134*

SkyLight Professional Development

Index

Library of Congress Online Exhibitions (Web site), 51
Lichtenstein, Roy (Web site), 126
Life and Times of William Shakespeare, The (Web site), 86, *87, 89, 90*, 94
Lincoln, Abraham, 141
Literature curriculum, using virtual field trips in, 108–13
Load time for Web sites, 57–58
Locations, geographic, Internet sites for, 108–09
Logical/mathematical intelligence, 64, *100*
Los Angeles Zoo, The (Web site), 20
Loysville Youth Development Center (Loysville, PA), 147
Lycos (search engine), 20, 25, 54, 119, 129

Maclachlan, Patricia, 109
Magritte, Rene, 126
Malcolm X, 116
Mapquest (Web site), 139
Marais des Cygnes State Historical Site (Web site), 143
Marsh, Reginald, 126
Mary Bradbury's Trial (Web site), 28
Massachusetts Emigrant Aid Society (Web site), 142
Massachusetts Enquirer, The (Web site), 31
Materials
    curricular, accessing via Internet, 11–13
    for virtual field trip, investigating, 152
Mathematics curriculum, using virtual field trips in, 123–25
Math Forum, The (Web site), 12, 31, 124
MathMagic (Web site), 13
Mayaquest (Web site), 20
Medieval and Renaissance Instruments (Web site), 84, *85, 89, 90*, 94

Medieval Art and Architecture (Web site), *85, 89, 90*, 94
Medieval Domestic Life (Web site), 146
Medieval English Literature (Web site), 83
Medieval/Renaissance Food Homepage (Web site), 84, *85, 89, 90*, 94
Medieval times, virtual field trip to, *134*, 145–46
Mega Math (Web site), 124
Merce: Biography (Web site), 129
Merce Cunningham Dance (Web site), 129
Metacrawler (search engine), 20, 26, 28, 47, 49, 50–51, 54, 79, 81, *82*, 83, 111, 112, 113, 114, 115, 118, 127, 128, 129, 152
Michelangelo, 126
Middle School Problem of the Week (Web site), 13
Miller, Arthur, 26, 35
Miro, Jean, 126
Mr. William Shakespeare and the Internet (Web site), 81, *82*, 86, 89, 90, 94
Monet, Claude, 126
Monterey Bay Aquarium (Web site), 20
Mozart, Wolfgang, 129
Multicultural studies, virtual field trip for studying, 118–19
Multiple intelligences, 62–64, 99, 100
    checklist, 100
Music, virtual field trips for studying, 128–29
Music of the Civil War (Web site), *55*
Musical/rhythmic intelligence, 64, *100*

Napoleonic era, virtual field trip on, 116
Napoleon Series: Life & Times of Napoleon Boneparte, The (Web site), 116
NASA Web site, 10–11, 113
National Council for the Teaching of Mathematics (NCTM), 125
Naturalist intelligence, 63, 64, *100*

SkyLight Professional Development

New England Information Network (Web site), 111
New York Times: The 1998 Tony Award Nominations (Web site), 128
NOBLE Web: Cinco de Mayo (Web site), 119

O'Dell, Scott, 108
Origin of the Name Jayhawkers, The (Web site), 142
Out of my town, virtual field trip to, *134*, 138–39

Packaged virtual field trips, 18–20
    commercial sites and, 18
    educational sites and, 18–19
    informational sites and, 18
Pacoima Middle School (Los Angeles, CA), 149
Parameters of virtual field trip, determining, 43–44, 73–74, 151
Past, Internet sites for studying the, 109–10
Personalized virtual field trips, 19–20
Petition of Accused Witch Mary Easty (Web site), 28
Picasso, Pablo, 126
Planetarium Sky Theater (Web site), 20
Poetry and Music of the Civil War (Web site), *55*
Poplar Forest (Web site), 106
Practicality of virtual field trip, 45–47
Preparation time for virtual field trip, 101–02

Quantrill's Flag (Web site), 143

Ragtime (Broadway musical), 127
Ragtime (Web site), 127, 128
Ragtime: The Musical (Web site), 127
Rain Forest Alliance Home Page (Web site), 49
Rain forest virtual field trip, 49–50
Rain Forests Directory, Rain Forests, Ecology, Directory, Guide, Yellow Pages, Index, . . . (Web site), 49

Ravensgard Medieval Homepage (Web site), 146
Ready-to-use virtual field trips, 133–50
Rebuilding of Shakespeare's Globe Theater (Web site), 81, *82*
Rembrandt, Harmensz van Rijn, 126
Remember the Maine (Web site), 116
Renior, Pierre-Auguste, 126
Rivera, Diego, virtual field trip to see artwork of, *134*, 147–48
Robert Frost: Three Volumes and C (Web site), 12
Rock and Roll Hall of Fame, The (Web site), 20
Rome, ancient, planning a virtual field trip on, 23–24
Romeo and Juliet, 71, 77, 99, 102
Roosevelt, Franklin Delano, 11–12
Roosevelt Presidential Library, 11
Rubric, constructing for virtual field trip, 99, *101*
Rundetaarn, The Round Tower (Web site), 106
Rural Impressions (Web site), 106

Salem, Massachusetts (Web site), 27
Salem, Massachusetts What about Witches? (Web site), 33
Salem Common (Web site), 28
Salem Massachusetts Architecture (Web site), 27
Salem@nationalgeographic.com (Web site), 32
Salem Witchcraft Trials of Salem Village, 1692, The (Web site), 33
Salem Witch Museum, The—Salem, Massachusetts (Web site), 27
Salem Witch Museum (Web site), 28
Salem Witch Museum Education–Salem, Massachusetts (Web site), 32
Salem Witch Trials: A Chronology of Events (Web site), 33, 34
Salem Woods (Web site), 28
Sarah, Plain and Tall (Maclachlan), 109
School-made Web sites, 49

SkyLight Professional Development

Index

Schrock, Kathy, 29, 52, 54, 83, 127, 152
Schuck, Robert, 149
Science curriculum, using virtual field trips in, 120
Scope of virtual field trip, determining, 43–44, 73–74
Search engines, 25–27
    using, 50, 79–82, 83–87
    versus directory, 28
Searching for a Web site, 54
Search time, reducing, 35
Seneca Elementary School (Seneca, MO), 135
Shakespeare, virtual field trip on, 71–102
Shakespeare, William, 71–102
Shakespearean Quest, A (Web site), 86
Shakespeare and Anti-Semitism: The Question of Shylock (Web site), 81, *82*
Shakespeare—Globe (Web site), 81, *82*
Shakespeare in Love (Web site), 80, *82*
Shakespeare Links on the Internet (Web site), 86
Shakespeare Magazine (Web site), 80, *82*
Shakespeare Page (Web site), 80, *82*
Shakespeare's Globe (Web site), 81, *82*, 89, 90, 94
Shakespeare the Man: His Life and Times (Web site), 86, *87*, *89*, *90*, 91
Shakespeare Web (Web site), 80, *82*
Sites, web. *See* Web site(s)
Slavery Timeline, A (Web site), 141
Smithsonian Institution, 11, 121
Social studies curriculum, using virtual field trips in, 113–16
Socrates, 14
Sondheim, Stephen, 128
Space exploration Web sites, 121
Spanish-American War, virtual field trip on, 116

Spider Glider—Science Museum of Minnesota (Web site), 136
Spider's habitat, virtual field trip to, *134*, 135–37
Spiders Home Page (Web site), 136
Spider Unit (Web site), 136
S. P. Q. R. Welcome to the Forum (Web site), 24
Statehood to 1900 (Web site), 143
Stephen A. Douglas (Web site), 141
Story of the Lincoln-Douglas Debates, The (Web site), 141
Structure of trip, creating, 59–60
Subject-matter sites
    comprehensive, 30–32
    specific, 32–33

Taj Mahal@ (Web site), 106
Teacher-created virtual field trips, 133–50
Teacher guest books, 33–35, 53, 54
Teacher lesson ideas for ready-made virtual field trips, *134*
Teacher's Guide to the Holocaust, A (Web site), 116
Teachers Helping Teachers (Web site), 23–24, 29, 34, 36, 52, 53, 54, 112, 127, 136, 152
Territorial Growth Map (Web site), 140
Theater, virtual field trips for studying, 127–28
Thumbnails of Spiders in NW Europe (Web site), 137
Thunderstone (search engine), 80
Tiger Information Center (Web site), 113
Time frame of virtual field trip, 59, 93–94
Time limits of trip, setting, 60
Timeline of Witch Trial History, A (Web site), 33
To Kill A Mockingbird (Lee), 108, 110
Tower of Pisa@ (Web site), 106
Turner, Joseph Mallord William, 126
Twain, Mark, 110

SkyLight Professional Development

Undersea and Oversee (Web site), 121
United States Capitol@ (Web site), 106
U.S. History (Web site), 30
Unofficial Visitors Guide to Gettysburg, The (Web site), 51
URL access, providing, 61
USA Today Weather (Web site), 8
Usefulness of Internet activities, 123

van Gogh, Vincent, 126
Verbal/linguistic intelligence, 64, *100*
Viability of virtual field trip, 45–47
Virtual field trip checklist, 66–67
Virtual Field Trips Site, The (Web site), 120
Virtual New England (Web site), 111
Visual arts, virtual field trips for studying, 126–27
Visual/spatial intelligence, 64, *100*

Warhol, Andy, 126
Weather Bureau, virtual field trip to, *134*, 149–50
Weather Information Superhighway—United States National Weather Bureau (Web site), 150
Web, creating a, 45, *46*
Webbing Process for a Virtual Field Trip Investigation, *48*
WebCrawler (search engine), 51, 80, 81, 113, 119, 129
Weber, Andrew Lloyd, 128

Web of possibilities, *75*, *78*, *88*
Web site(s)
    analyzing collected, 55–58, 87–91
    load time for, 57–58
    material, examining for appropriateness, 56
    school-made, 49
    searching for a, 54
Web Sites Related to Witchcraft Bibliography Project, 33
Welcome to MAIN STREET GETTYSBURG (Web site), 51
Welcome to Salem, Massachusetts (Web site), 27
Wharram: a look at peasants in the Middle Ages (Web site), 84, *85*, *89*, *90*, 94
White House, The, (Web site), 20
Wichamstow—a virtual Medieval village (Web site), 84, *85*, *89*, *90*, 94
William Quantrill and the Lawrence Massacre (Web site), 142
Witchcraft, Accused of (Web site), 27
Witchcraft Hysteria (Web site), 31
World Federation of Great Towers (Web site), 106
World Wide Arts Resources (Web site), 31, 114, 126–127
Writing curriculum, using virtual field trips in the, 112–13

Yahoo!, 20, 23, 24, 27, 28, 51, 54, 80, 81, 105–06, 109, 110, 111, 114, 115, 128, 139, 152
Yankee Web Explorer, The (Web site), 111
You Can—Spider Webs (Web site), 136

There are
one-story intellects,
two-story intellects, and three-story
intellects with skylights. All fact collectors, who
have no aim beyond their facts, are one-story men. Two-story men
compare, reason, generalize, using the labors of the fact collectors as
well as their own. Three-story men idealize, imagine,
predict—their best illumination comes from
above, through the skylight.
—*Oliver Wendell*
Holmes

PROFESSIONAL DEVELOPMENT

We Prepare Your Teachers Today for the Classrooms of Tomorrow

Learn from Our Books and from Our Authors!

Ignite Learning in Your School or District.

SkyLight's team of classroom-experienced consultants can help you foster systemic change for increased student achievement.

Professional development is a process not an event. SkyLight's experienced practitioners drive the creation of our on-site professional development programs, graduate courses, research-based publications, interactive video courses, teacher-friendly training materials, and online resources—call SkyLight Professional Development today.

SkyLight specializes in three professional development areas.

Specialty #1 Best Practices

We **model** the best practices that result in improved student performance and guided applications.

Specialty #2 Making the Innovations Last

We help set up **support** systems that make innovations part of everyday practice in the long-term systemic improvement of your school or district.

Specialty #3 How to Assess the Results

We prepare your school leaders to encourage and **assess** teacher growth, **measure** student achievement, and **evaluate** program success.

Contact the SkyLight team and begin a process toward long-term results.

2626 S. Clearbrook Dr., Arlington Heights, IL 60005
800-348-4474 • 847-290-6600 • FAX 847-290-6609
info@skylightedu.com • www.skylightedu.com